Praise for *The Alone Advantage*

"A primary trait in elite performers is their commitment to prepare. Terri shows you how to set yourself up for success by taking charge of your daily habits. This inspiring book will help you raise your personal standards and become the person you were born to be."

—Ed Mylett, global speaker, coach, entrepreneur, two-time bestselling author, and TV and podcast host

"In *The Alone Advantage* Terri shows us how to embrace our alone time and master our moments, which ultimately helps us to master our lives. I highly recommend reading this to achieve personal and professional success."

—Andrea Shaw, four-time Ms. Olympia

"This fast-moving, entertaining book is full of precious insights into success and happiness that you can apply immediately to set clear goals and priorities, use your time better, and start each day with greater energy and enthusiasm."

—Brian Tracy, speaker, author, and consultant

"Terri provides a unique perspective on the road to success, reminding us that our private moments of reflection can activate the strength within to win!"

—Les Brown, renowned motivational speaker, bestselling author, and radio and TV personality

"*The Alone Advantage* is a deep dive into how our private moments shape our success. Super inspiring and a must-read if you're into self-improvement and personal growth."

—Christy Wright, author, sp

"Terri Savelle Foy has masterfully tapped into a success principle that most goal-oriented achievers overlook. The simple principle of utilizing our time alone will transform your life. Anyone can experience temporary success, but Terri beautifully draws a step-by-step blueprint of success that can be implemented through simple application. Whether you have success, desire a greater level of success, or have never experienced success, this book is the secret key to the success you have been looking for!"
—Diana Scothorn, founder and president of The Benefit Link and author of *Daily Dose with Diana*

"*The Alone Advantage* teaches each of us the skills to hear God and help Him help us in our alone time with Him. Hear Terri Savelle Foy's heart as she passionately pushes us all to the uncomfortable place of listening only to our Master's voice in that void of outside pressures and influences. When you read this book, you will be touching your relationship with God in a profound and new way, establishing boundaries, and opening veins of imagination that are heaven-sent and destiny-driven."
—Stewart Scothorn, CEO of The Benefit Link

"An inspiring journey of self-discovery and transformation! In *The Alone Advantage*, Terri reveals what successful people do behind closed doors. This book is a compelling reminder that true success begins in the quiet moments when no one is watching. Highly recommended for anyone seeking growth and success as they develop habits in the unseen hours."
—Paula White-Cain, bestselling author, coach, pastor, and motivational speaker

"As I look back on my life as an entrepreneur, the most creative and powerful times were in those 'be still and know' moments. Terri has the special gift of knowing how to capture her audience and give them what they need: guidance, wise counsel, and inspiration. Her kindness, insight, and creative spirit make her one of a kind."
—Gigi Butler, entrepreneur, author, motivational speaker, and founder of Gigi's Cupcakes

"The joyful and engaging success of Terri Savelle Foy did not come without a plan and purpose. She now shares in her book *The Alone Advantage* the simple plan and the daily to-do list to greater success in every area of your life."

—Joni Lamb, cofounder,
vice president, and broadcaster at
Daystar Television Network

"After reading Terri's new book, *The Alone Advantage*, I can't even pick one favorite habit out of the ten because they are all pure gold! Terri has an amazing way of communicating and inspiring us all to reach our God-given potential. I absolutely love this book and know it's going to change so many lives!"

—Carly Patterson, US Olympic gold medalist,
author, and speaker

"High-level performers know mastery begins in the details. Terri maps her plan out step by step, with practical guidance on how to win your day by mastering small morning habits. This book is practical and applicable no matter what level you're playing at. *The Alone Advantage* is gonna take you from amateur to *pro!*"

—Steve Weatherford, Super Bowl champion,
CEO, and podcast host

"Terri does it again with *The Alone Advantage*, beautifully illustrating that what you do in the unseen hours will lead to crazy success. She provides a practical, step-by-step plan for self-discovery and empowerment inspired by God's Word. It will make you want to hang the Do Not Disturb sign on your door and start embracing your alone time. If you are looking to grow and take the next step to achieving your goals, this is a must-read!"

—Chris Goodman, president and
CEO of OpenRoad Lending

"It's true! Every big revelation from the Lord has come to me while I was alone: riding my bike, walking on the beach, reflecting by my pond, out on my motorcycle, or face down on the carpet with my Bible. Terri Savelle Foy knows that planning time to be by yourself is to your advantage. Your alone time is the secret sauce that will make you crazy successful in whatever you choose to do!"

—David Crank, author, speaker, and co-lead pastor of Faith Church

"I am recommending *The Alone Advantage* to everyone who is seeking personal and professional success! This book is filled with insights from a voice I've trusted and admired for nearly two decades. If you struggle with feeling stuck, tired of living each day as a repeat of the last, and you want change, this book is for you. As always, Terri brings step-by-step truths, direction, and purpose to achieve big results."

—Camille White, lead pastor of Hillsong France, Geneva, and Luxembourg

"Even cheerleaders need a cheerleader, and Terri has lifted our spirits in a personal, practical, and inspiring way."

—Kelli Finglass, speaker, director of the Dallas Cowboys Cheerleaders

"Terri always knows just the spot to hit so that you can take your life to the next level. That thing that everybody tries to get out of, but which is really the key to success, is some time alone with God. Instead of running to the phone, Terri reminds us that running to the throne is so important. Get this book, get your ears on, take Terri's journaling advice, and learn the keys to her success and how to apply them to your life!"

—Nicole Crank, host of *The Nicole Crank Show*, bestselling author, speaker, and co-lead pastor of Faith Church

the *Alone*
advantage

the *Alone*
advantage

10 Behind-the-Scenes Habits
That Drive Crazy Success

TERRI SAVELLE FOY

EMANATE
BOOKS

Published in Nashville, Tennessee, by Emanate Books, an imprint of Thomas Nelson. Emanate Books and Thomas Nelson are registered trademarks of HarperCollins Christian Publishing, Inc.

Author is represented by The Fedd Agency, Inc., P. O. Box 341973, Austin, Texas 78734 with respect to the literary work.

Thomas Nelson titles may be purchased in bulk for educational, business, fundraising, or sales promotional use. For information, please email SpecialMarkets@ThomasNelson.com.

Unless otherwise noted, Scripture quotations are taken from The Holy Bible, New International Version®, NIV®. Copyright © 1973, 1978, 1984, 2011 by Biblica, Inc.® Used by permission of Zondervan. All rights reserved worldwide. www.Zondervan.com. The "NIV" and "New International Version" are trademarks registered in the United States Patent and Trademark Office by Biblica, Inc.® Scripture quotations marked AMP are taken from the Amplified® Bible (AMP). Copyright © 2015 by The Lockman Foundation. Used by permission. www.lockman.org. Scripture quotations marked AMPC are taken from the Amplified® Bible (AMPC). Copyright © 1954, 1958, 1962, 1964, 1965, 1987 by The Lockman Foundation. Used by permission. www.lockman. org. Scripture quotations marked ESV are taken from the ESV® Bible (The Holy Bible, English Standard Version®). Copyright © 2001 by Crossway, a publishing ministry of Good News Publishers. Used by permission. All rights reserved. Scripture quotations marked GNT are taken from the Good New Translation in Today's English Version—Second Edition. Copyright 1992 American Bible Society. Used by permission. Scripture quotations marked HCSB are taken from the Holman Christian Standard Bible®. Copyright © 1999, 2000, 2002, 2003, 2009 by Holman Bible Publishers. Used by permission. HCSB® is a federally registered trademark of Holman Bible Publishers. Scripture quotations marked KJV are taken from the King James Version. Public domain. Scripture quotations marked MSG are taken from THE MESSAGE. Copyright © 1993, 2002, 2018 by Eugene H. Peterson. Used by permission of NavPress. All rights reserved. Represented by Tyndale House Publishers, Inc. Scripture quotations marked NASB are taken from the New American Standard Bible® (NASB). Copyright © 1960, 1962, 1963, 1968, 1971, 1972, 1973, 1975, 1977, 1995, 2020 by The Lockman Foundation. Used by permission. www.lockman.org. Scripture quotations marked NCV are taken from the New Century Version®. Copyright © 2005 by Thomas Nelson. Used by permission. All rights reserved. Scripture quotations marked NKJV are taken from the New King James Version®. Copyright © 1982 by Thomas Nelson. Used by permission. All rights reserved. Scripture quotations marked NLT are taken from the Holy Bible, New Living Translation. Copyright © 1996, 2004, 2015 by Tyndale House Foundation. Used by permission of Tyndale House Ministries, Carol Stream, Illinois 60188. All rights reserved. Scripture quotations marked NRSV are taken from the New Revised Standard Version Bible. Copyright © 1989 National Council of the Churches of Christ in the United States of America. Used by permission. All rights reserved worldwide.

All emphasis in Scripture quotations is added by the author.

Any internet addresses, phone numbers, or company or product information printed in this book are offered as a resource and are not intended in any way to be or to imply an endorsement by Thomas Nelson, nor does Thomas Nelson vouch for the existence, content, or services of these sites, phone numbers, companies, or products beyond the life of this book.

Library of Congress Cataloging-in-Publication Data

Names: Foy, Terri Savelle, author.
Title: The alone advantage : 10 behind-the-scenes habits that drive crazy success / Terri Savelle Foy.
Description: Nashville, Tennessee : Nelson Books, [2024] | Summary: "Twenty minutes a day with God can change everything. Through focused alone time and question-driven journaling, Terri Savelle Foy will guide readers to discover how God has equipped them for purpose, hope, and success"--Provided by publisher.
Identifiers: LCCN 2023029423 (print) | LCCN 2023029424 (ebook) | ISBN 9781400244997 (tp) | ISBN 9781400244980 (epub)
Subjects: LCSH: God (Christianity) | Time--Philosophy. | Success.
Classification: LCC BT153 .F59 2024 (print) | LCC BT153 (ebook) | DDC 231--dc23/eng/20231011
LC record available at https://lccn.loc.gov/2023029423
LC ebook record available at https://lccn.loc.gov/2023029424

Printed in the United States of America

24 25 26 27 28 LBC 6 5 4 3 2

I dedicate this book to four people.

First, to my dad, Jerry Savelle, for lovingly giving me the life-changing instruction to get alone. You taught me that God can't use me publicly until I get victory privately. What I used to dread has become what I most defend. What I thought would be awful and boring turned out to be amazing and exceptionally beneficial to every single area of my life.

Second, to John Maxwell. You are the one who opened my eyes to the seriousness of how we spend each twenty-four-hour day. You made me realize that our future is hidden in our daily agenda. I changed my routine, and it changed my whole life.

Third, to my husband, Rodney. With our marriage barely hanging on, you were the reason I was asked to get alone, temporarily. What we thought was the end of our marriage turned out to be the end of a rut, the end of repeating the same habits and mistakes, and the beginning of restoration and living our wildest dreams.

Fourth, to you, the reader, who is seeking direction for your life, wisdom from God, and a step-by-step plan to go after your dreams. You'll no longer try to prevent solitude; you'll protect it as you quickly discover this extraordinary advantage that drives crazy success.

Contents

Contents

PART 6: LINE UP!

PART 7: SPEAK UP!

PART 8: CHEER UP!

PART 9: STEP UP!

PART 10: GET UP!

Introduction

Have you ever wondered why successful people often spend time alone? Why they seek solitude or find inspiration in isolation? If you had told me years ago that I would write a book about the *advantage* of being alone, I would have argued that seclusion is a form of suffering. That's why solitary confinement is often used as a punishment. However, that naïve mindset kept me full of distractions and in a constant state of busyness—avoiding silence and stillness—and, as a result, failing to improve my life for over a decade.

Once I discovered that successful people do very specific things in private with nobody watching in order to succeed in public with everybody watching, I not only desired to spend time alone but also schedule that time, seek it out, and protect it. When people see the crazy success that God has given me and they ask how my life transformed so drastically, I always share my story of the alone advantage. We all like advantages. *Advantage* means "a condition or circumstance that puts one in a favorable or superior position."[1]

The average person does not spend time alone. The average successful person does. If you want to gain a favorable or superior position in life, find a Do Not Disturb sign, hang it on your door, and start doing what successful people do alone.

If the thought of being alone to hear from God, to reflect, to journal, and to gain insight bores you, maybe using a timer will make it more palatable. After all, it's not what we do occasionally that shapes our lives—it's what we do routinely. It's not a single two-hour workout that shapes your body—it's twenty minutes of exercise daily. It's not an all-day cleaning marathon that keeps your house tidy—it's twenty minutes of maintenance each night before you go to bed. It's not reading a full book in one day that shapes your mindset—it's twenty minutes of inspiration at the start of each day.

When I was a little girl, my mom would tell my sister and me to load the dishwasher, and even though we dreaded that awful chore, we found a way to make it fun. We set a timer. For some reason the thought of that little clock on the stove ticking down gave us the motivation and high-speed challenge of seeing just how fast we could pile in the plates.

Whether it's timing your commute to the office, timing how long a casserole takes, or timing your alone moments to discover your purpose, the minutes matter. In this book I'm going to show you how timing yourself in moments of silence will help you discover your purpose, your potential, and your passion in less time than it takes to finish an old episode of *Friends*.

Master your minutes in private, and you'll master your life in public.

. . .

I'm sitting in a beautiful, light-blue beach condo in sunny Florida, with the windows open, the palm trees waving in the breeze, joggers going by, and a bicycle leaning next to my front door. You can just feel the calm, relaxing air in the environment. Vacationers from the North are taking in this tropical weather, sitting in lounge chairs along the shore. Yesterday I watched a young man propose to his girlfriend outside a seaside restaurant on a candle-covered lawn. Everyone seems to be enjoying the weather, the lighthearted atmosphere, and each other's company.

But I forgot to mention. I'm all alone.

My husband left this morning after spending three days checking me in to this condo, stocking my kitchen full of groceries, and making sure the area was safe for me to stay by myself and write this book on *alone time*.

I cherished the three days with him here—holding hands as we walked to local cafes, sampling homemade pastries at the local farmers market, and then sharing a blanket at night on the couch as we watched whatever was free on the cable channel.

To be honest, when he waved goodbye this morning and I turned around to enter the empty condo, I had a moment of sadness at the thought of being here all by myself. Away from the world, nobody to talk to in person, sleeping alone, and making that my new normal for the next fifteen days.

But then I remembered that being alone is the secret to my success. Isolation is a luxury—if you do the right things.

What happens in private is far more important than what people see in public. In fact, the rewards, the blessings, and the incredible opportunities I've been given in my life today are a direct result of what I did behind the scenes yesterday.

Have you ever wondered what successful people do when nobody's watching? You've probably heard this famous quote attributed to Frank Ocean: "Work hard in silence, let success make the noise." This lines up with the phrase that changed my entire outlook on silence and solitude: "People are rewarded in public for what they practice in private."[2]

Your greatest ideas will come in isolation, your strength will be found in solitude, and your purpose will be discovered in privacy when nobody is around. In fact, God can't use you publicly until you get victory privately.

> The rewards, the blessings, and the incredible opportunities in my life are a direct result of what I did behind the scenes.

It's what happens behind closed doors in your private moments that leads to success in front of the crowd. Remember the story of David in the Bible? He single-handedly killed a lion and destroyed a bear in private with nobody watching, and that prepared him to kill a giant named Goliath in public with everyone looking (1 Samuel 17).

. . .

I haven't always felt so favorable about isolation. Years ago I had a defining moment in solitude that altered the entire direction of my life and inspired the writing of this book.

Let me give you the quick backstory leading up to this pivotal moment of isolation. Richard Branson claimed that "if it can't fit on the back of an envelope, it's rubbish."[3] So I'll shorten the past few decades as much as I can.

I grew up a very happy-go-lucky type of girl. I was a cheerleader all through high school, I was the homecoming queen, I earned my place in the National Honor Society, and I even dated the quarterback. My days were always filled with lots of activity and I was constantly surrounded by friends. It appeared that I had it all together in public, but I was hiding so much pain behind my big smile.

The back-of-the-envelope version is this: at fourteen years old I was violated and lost my virginity to a stranger on the floor of a fitness center. I felt so alone that night after I went to my grandmother's house. I bawled uncontrollably. I had such a poor self-image and crippling insecurities after that experience that I gradually fell into an abusive relationship with a guy for more than two years. He choked me, threw me in a ditch, and even banged my head against a steering wheel (many times). I felt so alone hiding all the abuse from my family and friends. Finally I ended that relationship, and while attending Texas Tech University—the last semester of my senior year—I got pregnant. I felt so alone, lying on my apartment floor in Lubbock, Texas, while scribbling this sentence in my journal: *I want to die.*

I forgot to mention that my dad is a minister, and the thought of him finding out what a letdown I had become filled me with enormous shame and guilt. I told my roommate, Theresa, that I wanted to run away and just head west. She said, "No, you're not." To add a little humor to my hopeless-looking life, she noted, "You don't even know which way is west" (which was true).

Instead I faced my reality and decided to marry the father of my baby. I borrowed my sister's wedding dress and walked down the aisle with my head held down in shame as my dad and Reverend Kenneth Copeland performed the shotgun wedding. Three weeks later the baby died. There I was, alone again—on a hospital bed having surgery to remove the baby.

Okay, that was an oversized envelope, but in summary I still graduated after that painful semester, we moved to Fort Worth, Texas, and I started working for my dad's organization.

And for the next eleven years my life was on autopilot.

A typical day looked like this: wake up at the last minute, jump in my car, take my little girl to school, sing all the way to the office, work eight hours, jump back in the car and pick up my little girl, sing on the way home, do my household chores, watch television for hours, feel overwhelmed when I went to bed, and get up to do it all again the next day.

For more than a decade my life was a constant routine of going nowhere. I paid my car note every month, my credit cards on the fifteenth, lived paycheck to paycheck, and had nothing in my savings account. My house was a bit of a mess, I was a mess, I had no vision for my life, and I had a little girl looking to me as a role model.

Until one day, I was alone.

I spent twenty minutes in solitude.

• • •

It was the year 2002, and I had been busier than ever. My husband and I both had full-time jobs, plus we had become part-time youth pastors at our local church.

As if running an entire media department wasn't keeping me busy enough, I was preparing messages every Wednesday night for a warehouse full of teenagers. In addition to weekend outings—including Six Flags Over Texas, disco bowling, and girls' night sleepovers at our house—there were also dance recitals and ballet practices for my daughter. It was an endless list of activities and to-do lists that were draining me and my husband.

At the end of the day, I would drive by the mailbox, collect the bills, and think, *Another thing to add to my list.* I would run a bath for my little girl, gather up all the towels and dirty clothes, toss them on the laundry room floor, and again think, *When am I going to do all this laundry?* Kindergarten field trips, Wednesday-night youth meetings, Tuesday-morning media brainstorming sessions, grocery shopping, bill paying, housecleaning, family time—everything was taking its toll on me and my marriage.

I was busier than ever, working harder than ever, investing in more people than ever, but neglecting myself. I was literally never alone. And I think subconsciously I was avoiding being alone. I didn't want to think about how messed up my marriage had gotten or how limited our finances had become or even how to get control of this overwhelm.

Until one day everything hit a breaking point. My husband and I decided to separate. On the verge of divorce, we resigned as youth pastors. My boss, who was also my dad, knew the emotional toll everything was taking on me, and he uttered these painful words: "I want you to temporarily work from home. *Alone.*"

That word *alone* represented so many negative reminders to me.

Alone in my bedroom, crying myself to sleep after being violated at the gym, represented severe rejection.

Alone on that dirt road after being thrown in the ditch represented a pathetic, easily controlled, insecure girl.

Alone on that apartment floor after discovering I was pregnant outside of marriage represented shame, disgrace, and humiliation.

Alone in that hospital bed after losing our baby represented sadness and loss.

Alone in this house after eleven years of busyness represented more than a decade of disappointment with where I'd ended up.

I didn't have a good track record with *alone*. And here I was being forced to embrace a season of solitude.

I remember driving home one dark and rainy night with my mind tormented by painful memories, confusion over my current circumstances, and regret over where my life had ended up. I couldn't walk into my house yet. I was hurting. I pulled into a cul-de-sac at the front of my neighborhood and just parked. I left the car running and leaned my head against the steering wheel and cried from the deepest part of my soul.

I felt so alone. It wasn't just the feeling of being alone in that car. I felt so alone in what I was facing. I felt like nobody would understand, nobody could help me, nobody could relate, and nobody could take my pain away.

I was the loneliest person in the world . . . inside.

No amount of advice or number of sermons could take away the loneliness I was feeling. When the friend left, the church service was over, or it was five o'clock at the office, I was still left alone to face the reality of my situation.

You may or may not necessarily feel physically alone in a room or an empty house, but your loneliness could be in the situation you're facing right now. You feel alone in the struggle, alone in your marriage, alone in your dreams, alone in your mind, alone in a rut.

I always hated to be alone. Even when I was a little girl, I would climb out of my bed and tiptoe into my sister's room and climb in bed with her. Somehow I felt safer knowing someone was there beside me.

> Many people fear being alone because they're forced to face what's going on in their minds.

I always wanted friends to spend the night or to just hang out with me. Even if we weren't engaging in a lot of conversation, I liked knowing someone was there.

Many people have a fear of being alone because when they are, they are forced to face what's going on in their lives and, more importantly, what's going on in their minds. When you're alone you discover what's turning around in your thoughts. And that can be very alarming!

Robin Sharma said,

Most people have all this pain and self-hatred deep within them and because they've never processed through that pain, they need to structure their life to be busy always doing things. . . . They are scared of being alone because when you're alone, you not only start thinking, you start feeling. And that is hard and uncomfortable, but that's where you grow.[4]

During this painful season I took a weekend trip to visit my friend Jodi in New Orleans. She knew about my separation and encouraged me to get away for some girl time. After three days of trying all the Cajun food I could manage, her dad, evangelist Jesse Duplantis, shared some advice that shifted my outlook on what to do next. First, he told me to stop looking at my husband's problems and all the mistakes in our marriage, and then he uttered this gently blunt four-word command: "You. Work. On. You!"

Not long after that I heard Joyce Meyer say that God *will* change your circumstances, but He'll change you first.[5] Then I came across an anonymous quote: "If you want the future to change, you've got to change."

I thought, *Why is everyone pointing at me?!* But I took the words to heart.

When I first received my dad's direction to work from home—*alone*—I could feel anxiety rise in my body. Just the thought of not being around people during that time in my life and having to spend every day in my empty house was completely dreadful. I remember day one of working from home. I got up at 5:00 a.m. and went for my daily walk to cry out to God. I was hurting so badly inside. I walked and prayed for twenty minutes, went back to the house, and got ready. I woke up my daughter and took her to school. After dropping her off, I was crying as I pulled away from the elementary building. I didn't want to be without her. I needed someone with me.

I drove home, fearing the walk into that empty house and facing the reality that the life I once loved had changed so much and I was not the person I thought I would be by this time. I had no dreams. I had no goals to pursue. I was miserable. I walked in through the back door, laid my keys on the kitchen counter, and looked around thinking, *What do I do now?*

I set a timer for twenty minutes. The timer forced me to stay focused for a set time, yet twenty minutes did not feel like an overwhelming chunk of time.

What I did next became my lifetime morning routine.

And it led to many life changes:

- Enjoying a restored marriage (thirty-two years together)
- Regularly depositing money in the bank
- Founding an organization
- Writing fifteen books
- Launching a TV show

- Speaking at some of the largest conferences in the world
- Purchasing offices and hiring teams of people
- Developing courses that reach thousands of people in more than 150 nations
- And having the opportunity to rent a condo on a beach in Florida to tell you all about what successful people do in private so they are rewarded in public

If you're in a rut, I am going to show you how to get out.

If you're so busy you barely have time to read this book, I am going to help you get control of your schedule with a twenty-minute challenge.

If you're confused about what God wants you to do with your life, this book will give you action steps to discover your purpose.

If you're frustrated and wondering if there's more to life, this book will confirm that you haven't seen your best days yet.

And if you're afraid of stepping out and going after your scariest dreams, this book will give you the boost of courage to never shrink back in fear but pursue every God-given dream in your heart. "And your Father, who sees what you do in private, will reward you" (Matthew 6:4 GNT).

Your strength will be found in solitude.

Your ideas will come in isolation.

Your purpose will be discovered in privacy.

All it takes is a twenty-minute timer and you. Alone.

PART 1

Listen Up!

CHAPTER 1
Hear the Music

Make time to be alone. Your best ideas live within solitude.
—ROBIN SHARMA

There was a man in a pair of jeans, a plain T-shirt, and sneakers playing the violin during rush hour in the middle of an underground metro station in Washington, DC. A hidden camera was set up to watch how the thousands of pedestrians reacted to his concert. The musician played six incredible pieces by Bach. One person paused to listen while another tossed money to him. Some threw quarters, dimes, and pennies.

Children seemed to be the most interested in his performance. The *Washington Post* reported, "Every single time a child walked past, he or she tried to stop and watch and every time, a parent scooted the kid away."[1] During the forty-five minutes he played, only six listeners paused their commute to hear his music. Many passersby spoke loudly on their cell phones so they could be heard over the noise of the violinist.

When he finally stopped playing that day, no one noticed and no one applauded. There was complete silence. Only two days before this, the vagabond-looking violinist had a sold-out performance in Boston where the ticket price averaged one hundred dollars. But nobody in the metro knew that the man was Joshua Bell, the world-famous violinist, playing one of the most difficult pieces composed for the violin, Bach's Partita No. 2, on an $8.5 million Stradivarius violin![2]

What will we miss in life if we're so focused and busy we don't notice or stop to enjoy when one of the world's best musicians plays one of the world's most difficult pieces?

Getting away from all the distractions vying for your attention and just listening will be the most challenging and rewarding thing you will ever do to discover your purpose. It is truly the greatest private habit of the most successful people in the world. They make time to stop and listen.

Most of us avoid immersing ourselves in solitude, like I did, because it's where we uncover everything.

The market is always fighting for your undivided attention. The average person spends their day with so much noise. We get on Instagram before we get out of bed. We turn on our playlist as we turn on the coffeepot. We chat at the watercooler. We return home and check out who got engaged after the rose ceremony while simultaneously checking Facebook—until it's time to go to bed and start the process again the next morning. We spend most of our time listening to others' voices and rarely our own, much less the voice of God.

> Getting away from the distractions and just listening will be the most challenging and rewarding thing you do to discover your purpose.

The thought of spending time alone without checking YouTube or having Netflix on in the background can feel like torture. Some people would rather be physically harmed than sit alone quietly in a room for twenty minutes to think.

Bob Beaudine said, "Once you meet with God, you'll discover something amazing. You'll find out He does more than just listen to you; He has a plan—plans to prosper you, give you hope, and always shed light on your great future. But to know these plans you have to stop and listen."[3]

When you look at the great geniuses the world has known, they all have one thing in common: they spent a lot of time alone thinking. In the Bible most people got their vision out in the hills, the deserts, the wilderness, in the quiet place of solitude. Jesus spent time alone. Paul spent time alone. Moses spent time alone. "But Jesus Himself would often slip away to the wilderness and pray [in seclusion]" (Luke 5:16 AMP). Alone is where you receive direction, clarity, answers, wisdom, and confidence.

I heard someone say there are two reasons we find it agonizing to spend time alone: either we get bored easily, or we want to avoid the reality of where our life has ended up. I was the latter. I didn't want to be honest with myself or with God about how confused I was or how disappointed I felt with where I had landed in life (because of my own choices). But being alone proved to be the absolute best thing that could have ever happened to me.

You might be asking, "But what do I do when I'm alone?" Let me point out that you will need two items that will prove to be the greatest tools on your road to success: a journal and a pen.

. . .

I'll never forget that first morning in 2002 when I began the "forced" habit of aloneness at the direction of my boss. After dropping off my daughter at school, I drove home, walked into my kitchen, lit a green-tea-scented candle (I can almost smell it today), grabbed an empty journal and a blue pen, and plopped myself on the sofa. I set a timer for twenty minutes, which sounded like an eternity, and just sat there. The stillness of the room was frightening. It annoyed me greatly to not have noise in the background—not the TV, music, someone on the phone, the neighbor mowing their lawn, the garbage truck collecting bins, birds chirping—seriously nothing other than quietness.

I had never practiced the art of doing nothing.

It felt like time was being stretched.

I couldn't remember the last moment I'd truly sat down and listened for that still, small voice. I stared at the blank page of that journal and began writing my thoughts. I was shocked. The more I wrote, the more sincere and honest I was about my feelings.

Why is my marriage falling apart?
What led me to making poor decisions that resulted in this
    miserable state of mind?
Why am I so angry?
Why do I hide my feelings even from those I love the most?
Why am I so insecure and inferior?
How did I slide into this exhausting rut?
What do I really want to do with my life?

The more I penned my thoughts in the following days, the deeper I dove into my reality. I found so much healing on the pages of those journals. I wrote out scriptures that brought peace to my tormented mind. I became aware of people I needed to forgive and saw how my weaknesses were overpowering my strengths. I came face-to-face with the truth that I had never really given myself permission to dream. I realized that my insecurities stemmed from not ever thinking I was enough.

We need these consistent times in solitude. It's almost like self-therapy. It's where introspection happens as you become more aware of . . . you. It's almost as if you become your own counselor when you get honest with your deepest thoughts.

Many people say, "Don't just sit there, *do something*!" I always say, "Don't just do something, *sit there*—and listen. And *then* write in your journal."

How good are you at being alone? How often do you hear nothing? When was the last time you sat quietly by yourself and just thought? *About what, Terri?* Life. Your future. Where you are headed.

Where you see yourself five years from now. What you really want. What you want to change. What's bothering you. Who you need to forgive. What you need to stop doing. What you need to pursue. What God is speaking to your heart.

Perhaps, like me years ago, you haven't been still long enough to ask yourself those vital questions and—more importantly—to obtain answers, because you're never alone. Maybe you even pray, like I did every morning, but you never listen for God to communicate back to you.

Make Time to Think

Carmine Gallo described what happened when "one day in 1966, two men met for drinks at the hotel's bar. One was a Texas businessman; the other a chain-smoking, whiskey-swigging lawyer."[4] Herb Kelleher and Rollin King met that day to discuss business ideas they'd been entertaining. On this particular day, they sat at the table and thought about their future and the ideas rolling around in their heads. What did they want to do, to create, to start? One of them picked up a cocktail napkin, flipped it over, and drew a triangle. "At the top of the triangle they wrote 'Dallas,' on the bottom left 'San Antonio,' and on the bottom right 'Houston.' Their vision was simple—to create a small, local airline connecting three Texas cities."

That business plan that they sat there quietly thinking about, sketched on the back of a hotel napkin, would wind up impacting the lives of millions of Americans. On March 15, 1967, Herb and Rollin established

> *Thought* is the original source of all wealth, all success, all material gain, all great discoveries and inventions and all achievement.
> —CLAUDE M. BRISTOL

Southwest Airlines. And I love that the original napkin is framed in the Dallas headquarters. "Southwest is the world's largest airline, employing 46,000 people, carrying more than 100 million passengers a year, and generating billions of dollars of quarterly profit."[5] Makes me want to pick up a napkin and start drawing!

. . .

The chairman of Chick-fil-A, Dan Cathy, has reported spending half a day every two weeks and one solid day each month alone to think. He allocates fifteen to twenty minutes to solitude before starting each day.[6]

One synonym for *think* is *meditate*. For some people, *meditate* is a bad word because they associate it with New Age religions. There are many types of meditation, but I'm referring to it in the context of a believer's devotional life. The Bible uses the word *meditate* eighteen times in the New International Version.[7] God wants you to meditate. He even explains that meditation is a part of your journey to success: "Keep this Book of the Law always on your lips; meditate on it day and night, so that you may be careful to do everything written in it. Then you will be prosperous and successful" (Joshua 1:8).

Meditation is a critical aspect of prayer. Prayer is you talking; meditation is you listening! Most people never meditate—I didn't. I did all the talking when I prayed. Most people tell the Lord what's on their hearts, plead for things, and then prayer is over. Your dream is never revealed to you while you're talking. You must be quiet and just listen. You'll be amazed how loudly God speaks.

God wants to give you the healing, the wisdom, the direction you so desperately desire. He wants to reveal His next steps for your life and even give you those God-inspired ideas that produce great wealth. He wants to whisper insights and creative concepts, but you must get quiet to hear them.

Many successful people are committed to having meditation time every single day. They don't fear solitude; they embrace it. They schedule alone time. It's their moment to reflect, to recoup, to replenish their energy and to relate with the Lord. "Call to me and I will answer you, and tell you great and unsearchable things" (Jeremiah 33:3).

Just imagine what a simple twenty-minute habit of listening could produce in your life. After a month, that's ten hours that could lead to potentially hearing God-inspired ideas that produce a wealth of income, knowing which person to marry without hesitation, which deal to close without doubt, which project to launch without confusion. Imagine providing solutions for your company that bring significant promotion. Imagine being in the right places at the right times to make the right connections—all from a simple twenty-minute routine. This is why successful people spend time alone. There's great insight in isolation.

Michael Todd, author of *Crazy Faith*, wrote, "When you pray, withdraw. Even Jesus, the Son of God, had to intentionally get away from the noise."[8] It's time to stop, hear the music in your heart, and write.

CHAPTER 2

5 Things Successful People Write in Their Journals

A life worth living is a life worth recording.
—JIM ROHN

Years ago I received a letter from a sweet lady who heard I was speaking at a church near her home in Tyler, Texas. She was in a season where she was just stuck. She had lost hope and vision for her life and didn't have any goals to pursue. Every day felt like a vicious cycle of lather, rinse, and repeat. And she was miserable.

She felt like she was supposed to come to hear me speak, but she talked herself out of it. She was feeling down and didn't want to drive by herself, so she stayed home. But she knew she was still supposed to hear the message and ended up watching the conference online.

This woman heard me talk about the importance of keeping a journal, so she bought one and started writing. God began to remind her of dreams she'd forgotten. But she thought those dreams were hopeless. It was too late. She had wasted too much time. Those were *her* thoughts, however, not God's.

One of her dreams was to go back to school and become a nurse. Each morning as she spent time alone in prayer, her vision came alive in her, and at thirty-two years old she made a change! She went back to school, earned her degree, got her nursing certificate, and is now a full-time hospice nurse and loves her life.

Jim Rohn, who was a strong advocate for journaling, said, "If you're serious about becoming a wealthy, powerful, sophisticated, healthy, influential, cultured and a unique individual—keep a journal."[1] The reason that Rohn believed in the importance of writing things down is simply because you'll forget. You can't trust your memory. When you hear something valuable, write it down. When you stumble across something important, meaningful, or inspiring, write it down. When you feel like God is speaking to you in prayer, write it down. When you need clarity and direction for your life, write it down.

Let's look at five of the most powerful reasons to keep a journal.

1. Record Your Ideas

Many of us have experienced thinking of a great idea but before we considered writing it down, it was gone. In the business world, success coaches advise their clients to capture their thoughts and ideas in writing as soon as possible. Research indicates that any new ideas not captured *within thirty-seven seconds* are likely never to be recalled. *In seven minutes*, the ideas are gone forever![2]

Singer and designer Jessica Simpson has used her journal for songwriting ideas. She once said, "It is very, very therapeutic. There is a lot about heartbreak, there is a lot about perseverance. I used it as inspiration for my album. I used certain journal excerpts from certain journal entries. It has been an awesome experience for me."[3]

Ideas are all around you. Creative ideas will come to you at the most random times. Documenting these ideas in your journal could provide a solution or a breakthrough. Putting your ideas on paper ensures you have them recorded and you can start developing plans to put into action.

11

2. Identify Your Thoughts

Writing in a journal can help you express your thoughts. It becomes a tool for self-improvement. You truly get to know yourself more when you pinpoint your thoughts and feelings in writing. You'll be able to identify what is holding you back, what you're struggling to overcome, and the reasons behind your decisions.

Your private journal is a safe space where you can be honest with yourself. It's important you don't write with the intent of someone reading it. When I was in college I always kept a journal. When I did something I wasn't proud of, I would write in French. I knew nobody else in Lubbock, Texas, spoke French, so I could never be found out!

Your journal is very intimate, and you can reveal yourself with no restraints about who you really are and what you truly want.

Keeping a journal helps empty your brain of all the thoughts going through your head at any given time. When you need to make big decisions for your life such as where to move, which job to take, who to marry, where to apply, when to open your business, which university to attend, which offer to accept, just getting your thoughts out of your head and onto paper will help you make better decisions. Journaling has been shown to improve emotional health, mental health, and even reduce stress, which improves your physical health.

Actor Joseph Gordon-Levitt said, "I like to write. I've gone through different phases in my life of writing in a journal more or less frequently, but it's something I turn to, especially when I'm trying to work through something that's vexing me." He also said that journaling helps lead him to new answers or conclusions.[4]

3. Find Clarity

Clarity comes from questions. When you sit quietly and begin asking yourself tough questions, you will gain understanding as you write your responses to these uncertainties. I love what Gary Keller said: "You may be asking, 'Why focus on a question when what we really crave is an answer?' It's simple. Answers come from questions, and the quality of any answer is directly determined by the quality of the question."[5]

A few years ago I felt uneasy inside. I was stressed out, overworked, and feeling miserable with my current schedule. Finally, I sat quietly with my journal and began asking myself specific questions concerning my state of mind.

As I focused on answering each inquiry, I was able to identify my solution. Each curious sentence compelled me to dig deeper and find the answer, which pointed me in an entirely new direction. Had I not journaled that experience, I would still be running in circles wondering why.

If you lack clarity and direction in some aspect of your life, if you feel stuck in a certain season, if you're going through a major transition or feeling great stress in your current situation, ask yourself these questions and then write out your answers:

- What advice would you give to someone in your situation?
- What do you want to do?
- What would make the situation better?
- What actions do you need to take to change things?
- What are you doing wrong?
- What are you doing right?

With distractions all around, the best thing you can do is schedule time to be alone, get out your journal, and ask yourself questions. An article on Lifeline agrees: "Writing about challenging experiences can also help you process them in a constructive way, making it easier to handle difficult emotions. By engaging with your thoughts and feelings in this way, journaling can be a powerful tool for developing self-awareness and enhancing your mental health."[6]

If you're hazy about an issue in your life, write it out. This will help you make tough decisions. Instead of keeping those thoughts going around in circles in your head, pen them on paper. Start listing the consequences of each decision. What are the pros and cons? List every possible outcome of the choice you need to make.

4. Plan Your Future

This is where I began getting honest with myself about my future. I'll explain much more about this vital habit in part 5. As you sit quietly and create your ideal life on paper, it is like programming your GPS in your car—you've given yourself a clear map to follow.

You may have seen the famous TED talk "Living Beyond Limits,"[7] but if you haven't, let me tell you the story about a girl named Amy Purdy. At nineteen, she was working as a massage therapist, healthy, and active in snowboarding. One day Amy thought she had the flu, just like anybody would who has a low fever and body aches. But she got sicker and sicker as the hours passed until a cousin rushed her to the hospital.

It was nearly too late, as the doctors gave her only a 2 percent chance of survival from what was eventually diagnosed as bacterial meningitis. She was put on life support as her organs shut down, her body experiencing septic shock. But, by the grace of God, "the doctors were able to perform emergency surgery and saved Amy's life. Her legs, however, had to be amputated below the knees a few weeks later."[8]

After an intense recovery, Amy told Carmine Gallo for his book *The Storyteller's Secret*,

My darkest days were when I went home and had to walk in these metal legs for the first time. I had to rethink the rest of my life. I felt so out of control. I was at the bottom of the barrel. I was sick and tired of being sick and tired. That's when this question popped into my head: *If my life were a book and I was the author, how would I want the story to go?*

I knew what I didn't want. I didn't want people to feel sorry for me. I didn't want people to see me as disabled. I wanted to live a life of adventure and stories. This question allowed me to daydream; daydream about traveling the world, daydream about snowboarding, daydream about all the things I wanted to do and completely believing that it was possible.[9]

And that's exactly what Amy has proven. She won the bronze medal in snowboarding at the 2014 Paralympic Games, then became a finalist on *Dancing with the Stars*. And millions of people have watched her incredibly inspiring TED talk.

When was the last time you sat quietly and just thought about your vision, dream, and purpose? You don't have to do this only when something tragic or life-altering happens, though for most of us that's when we come to grips with life. Our future. Our choices. The direction our lives are going.

Think about Amy's story. And never underestimate the power of a blank book. Just like any habit, the more you practice it, the more comfortable you get doing it. It will become something you desire doing because you realize the impact it has on every aspect of your life.

Your journal is your personal space to ponder and pen your aspirations. The pages inside become your road map for success.

5. Hear from the Lord in Prayer

Starting your day in prayer sets the tone for the day. We can have devotions, go to church, and listen to messages, but nothing replaces hearing from God.

But Terri, how do you know if it's God? Practice. In 2002 I wasn't sure if it was God, but I practiced writing down whatever I heard. It's no different from when your best friend calls on the phone when you have caller ID blocked. You probably don't have to ask, "Who is this?" No, you recognize your friend's voice because you have practice hearing it. It's the same with God.

"Thus says the LORD God of Israel: 'Write in a book all the words which I have spoken to you'" (Jeremiah 30:2 AMP). God instructed Jeremiah to write down His words to His people. Why? Again, because we forget. We also can write down our conversations with God so we don't forget. Warning: If you've never journaled your thoughts before or practiced hearing from the Lord, you will have to fight the doubts in your head telling you that God speaks only to ministers but not to you. Those doubts are lies. God wants you to hear His voice more than anything.

Don't overthink your writing. Don't allow doubt to stop you from writing what you hear inside. Just write whatever is on your mind. The words are not intended to be a polished article. They're your thoughts and your impressions from the Lord. "I will instruct you and teach you in the way you should go; I will counsel you with my loving eye on you" (Psalm 32:8).

A friend of mine told me a true story about a lady sitting in church one Sunday morning. Suddenly she felt the Lord tell her to pledge $1,000 for their outreaches and to send it within thirty days. She was a single mom and did not have an extra $1,000 to donate. She sat there thinking, *God, where am I going to get that kind of money and that quickly?* But she wrote down her pledge and put it in the offering.

While she was spending time alone in prayer, God reminded her of something she had forgotten. The previous Christmas, when she didn't have the money to buy presents for her family and friends, she got creative. She handmade beautiful barrettes and hairbows and gave them as gifts. Her friends loved them. Remembering this, she thought, *I'll make some more.*

Next she was reminded of a friend who owned a boutique. *I wonder if she would allow me to sell some of my creations at her store.* She made a phone call, and the boutique owner said, "Sure, you can set up a booth this weekend."

The next Saturday morning, she was sitting there displaying her product, selling hairbows and barrettes one at a time, when one customer picked up a certain style, flipped it over, flipped it back, and examined it thoroughly. The customer put it down, picked up another one, and did the same. Over and over, one after another, she continued this routine. Finally, she asked if they were handmade and was assured they were. The curious inspector said, "Great. I'll take fifty thousand." She was a buyer for Nordstrom department store!

God-inspired ideas in prayer can change your destiny.

The Bible says His "sheep follow him because they know his voice" (John 10:4). God expects you to hear from Him. It's not strange. It's not mystical. It's not creepy. It's quite the opposite. It provides clarity, confidence, peace, comfort, direction, wisdom, and ideas for your life.

Admittedly, I've never heard an audible voice in prayer. What I've heard is more like an impression on the inside. My dad always said, "Whatever comes up in your spirit, just write it down."

During these consistent, scheduled times alone with the Lord, I've received the direction to start a ministry, to organize mission trips to France, to launch a women's conference, and even to name the conference ICING. It's in these times of solitude that I've overcome deep-rooted insecurities and built up my self-image enough to be able to stand on stages in front of thousands of people. It's behind closed doors with nobody around where I've given myself permission to dream up where I want to be tomorrow. It's in isolation where I mustered up the strength of character to forgive my husband and forgive myself and see my marriage completely restored.

"Be still and know that I am God" (Psalm 46:10). It all begins, and continues to this day, in my quiet times alone with a journal and a pen.

CHAPTER 3

Get Serious Behind Closed Doors

*I thought loving solitude was bad until I
discovered a whole new world in it.*
—MAXIME LAGACÉ

Lisa was diagnosed with dyslexia as a young woman. Her English teacher told her, "You are the weakest writer I have ever had in my class in my entire life." Her speech teacher told her, "I do not recommend that you ever speak in public; in fact, you need a desk job."

She grew up with those negative words impacting her life, filling her with insecurities and inferiorities—plus she was surrounded by gangs and violence in South Central LA. However, her Prince Charming came along, she fell in love, quickly got pregnant, and had her precious little boy.

When Lisa's son was only eight months old, her dream guy (so she thought) landed in jail. She was left destitute with only twelve dollars to her name. Lisa described this moment as the worst day of her life. She had to ask herself difficult questions such as: *Do I buy diapers for my baby or do I buy food for us?* She never forgot that helpless feeling that marked her for the rest of her life.

One day as she was wrapping her baby in bathroom towels because she couldn't afford diapers, Lisa had a defining moment. She rubbed his little tummy and uttered the heart-wrenching promise: "Mommy will *never* be this broke or this broken ever again."

That day she got serious about her future—behind closed doors.

Lisa said, "The reason people won't become who they want is because they are too attached to who they've been. You've got to rescue you first."[1] And that's exactly what she did.

She turned her little walk-in closet into her sanctuary, her private quarters, her quiet place. She bought mirrors for $2.99 at CVS and hung them up to make the closet look bigger. She would sit there from six thirty until midnight most nights—reading, journaling, learning, and investing in herself.

Lisa said, "I had to first commit to myself. I had to be willing to invest in me."

She'd give her son toys to play with, take the batteries out to confuse him for a while, and buy more quiet time. She didn't know how to make money, how to change her identity, or how to improve her life, so she looked for people who did. She started reading their books, listening to messages, going to conferences, taking courses. She said, "I went to the same conference forty-two times because I wanted to get it drilled in me. I wanted to finish their sentences."

That little girl, whose teacher said she was the weakest writer she had ever met, has now written seven books that have been translated into twenty languages. That little girl whose speech teacher said she should never speak in public is one of the most sought-after motivational speakers in the world. That young mother who had only twelve dollars to her name is now worth millions of dollars.

Lisa Nichols got serious and changed the entire direction of her life behind closed doors.[2]

Get Your Room Ready

It is important that you designate a room in your house that brings peace to you. And make that your room, your spot, your special place to get quiet, even if it's a closet. If you go into a room desiring to hear from God and that space is disorganized, junky, and cluttered, you're likely going to focus more on what needs to be cleaned up than you are on hearing from the Lord.

T. L. Osborn said, "Tranquility produces creativity."[3] Clean up your surroundings. Create a space that welcomes the Holy Spirit, that brings peace to your mind and removes anything competing for your attention.

My dad said to imagine the Holy Ghost as a holy guest in your home. How would you want your room to look if someone you considered a holy guest were to walk in? In other words, if you knew someone like Joyce Meyer, Joel Osteen, or your pastor were coming to your house today, how would you want to present that room? In what condition would it need to be for you to not feel embarrassed, ashamed, or humiliated? Whatever your answer, get it "show ready."

> Create a space that welcomes the Holy Spirit, that brings peace to your mind and removes anything competing for your attention.

A few years ago I was speaking at a conference in Denver, Colorado, and when I walked into the speaker's room, I gasped! It was my first introduction to my host, and I was shocked at how well she knew my style, my taste, and my favorite *everything.* Everywhere I looked, she had creatively placed little displays of "Terri."

On one table sat a gorgeous vase of blooming pink roses. Pink—my signature color. Another table was scattered with miniature Eiffel Towers and dozens of mouthwatering cupcakes piled high with pink buttercream icing.

Several copies of my books were enlarged and displayed on the stage. The sanctuary doors, restroom doors, and exits were covered in wallpaper displaying picturesque scenes of the City of Light (Paris, France). French music was playing in the hospitality room, and some women were even wearing French couture. I was truly overwhelmed by their hospitality and the detailed preparation for my arrival. Bottom line, I felt so welcomed.

You don't have to get this creative, but you can create an atmosphere for your heavenly Father that causes Him to feel welcome and that is conducive for you to hear His voice.

Get Your Heart Ready

In addition to clearing the clutter, you may need to empty out the junk from your past. When we hold on to debilitating emotions such as unforgiveness, sin, strife, anger, bitterness, shame, and guilt, it blocks our ability to hear from God. This could be the very reason you feel as if there's a wall between you and God, and you can't hear Him clearly.

For example, have you ever walked into someone's house and you just knew there'd been a fight? You didn't hear the argument, you didn't see the dishes flying, you didn't witness the uproar, but somehow you could sense an awkwardness in the atmosphere. What are you inclined to do in a situation like that? Get out as soon as possible! The house may look like a museum on the outside, but the spiritual atmosphere stinks on the inside!

The Holy Spirit is just as uncomfortable in an unclean, strife-filled heart. The solution to decluttering your heart is to simply repent. Get free from anything that's separating you from God. All you need to do is ask the Lord to forgive you for anything that displeased Him and brought shame and guilt into your life. Here's the good news: God forgives you the first time you ask. And He removes your sin as far as the east is from the west (Psalm 103:12). His forgiveness is instant, and it opens the door for Him to walk right in and feel at home in your presence.

When Isaiah sensed his sin (uncleanness) in God's presence, he said: "Woe to me! . . . I am ruined! For I am a man of unclean lips, and

I live among a people of unclean lips, and my eyes have seen the King, the LORD Almighty" (Isaiah 6:5). The scripture goes on to explain that an angel touched his lips, and his guilt was taken away. I love what verse 8 says: "Then I heard the voice of the Lord."

After he was cleansed of his sin, Isaiah heard the Lord speak. You may have experiences from your past that are still tormenting your mind and you've never come before God and repented. Ask Him to forgive you right now. Don't go another day with that clutter on the inside of you.

"Draw near to God and He will draw near to you" (James 4:7–8 NKJV). In other words, you make the first move. God is such a gentleman that He waits for you to take the first step. You take a step closer to God and He'll take one closer to you.

Get a Journal

Choose whatever type of journal you love the most. It can be a simple spiral notebook from your local convenience store, a luxurious leather notebook, or a plush pink journal that says "Dream Big." Use whatever works for you.

Richard Branson shared that he wouldn't have been able to build the Virgin enterprises without a simple notebook, which he takes with him wherever he goes.[4] Years ago, the Greek shipping magnate Aristotle Onassis said, "Always carry a notebook. Write everything down. . . . That is a million-dollar lesson they don't teach you in business school!"[5]

Get Ready to Write

Typically, whatever impression comes up in your heart is something God is dealing with you about. You may even hear only one word:

Forgive. Rest. Give. Stop. Freedom. Embrace. Discipline. One word can provide more direction for your life than an entire journal of random thoughts.

One year, I heard the word *invest.* So I wrote it down. I researched the word *invest* in the dictionary and discovered it means "to allocate money (or sometimes another resource, such as time) in the expectation of some benefit in the future"[6] and "to use, give, or devote (time, talent, etc.) for a purpose or to achieve something."[7] All year that one single word became my decision maker. When an opportunity arose, I was constantly reminded to invest. I invested in relationships, in family, in education, and in finances. *Invest* became my driving force all year long.

I remember one Sunday when I was invited to attend a twenty-five-year church anniversary service for some pastors who were longtime friends. It was quite a distance from my home, and it was my only weekend to be home in a long time. I wanted to rest that day, but the church invited me to attend the celebration so, using the word *invest* as my decision maker, I chose to drive the distance and invest my time.

Little did I know that God was setting *me* up to be extremely blessed! Before I left the church service to honor these precious pastors, they said, "Terri, we see what you're doing to impact lives in the nation of France, and we want to give an offering into your missions outreach to the French people. Here's a check for $5,000." *What? I went to honor them, and they blessed me?!* I simply went in obedience to my word from the Lord in prayer, but God honored it.

Since then, those same pastors have sponsored our annual ICING women's event, bringing young women in from safe houses and girls' homes by donating $20,000! All because I allowed one word scribbled in my journal to become my motivation for making decisions. God honored it.

I could tell you story after story of those same types of experiences.

One single word that you hear in your quiet time can shape you, stretch you, and provide the direction you need for an entire year. Sometimes that's all it takes to give you laser-like focus for the key areas of your life.

Get a Routine

I want you to have this phrase memorized and ingrained in your thinking: *The secret of your future is hidden in your daily routine.* It's not what you do occasionally that shapes your life, it's what you do consistently. Set aside a certain time every day to listen, to think, and to write in your journal, even if it's only five minutes. Five minutes is better than no minutes. And five minutes over the course of a year is more than thirty hours of practicing one of the private habits of the most successful people in the world.

I prefer to start my morning with this habit because it clears my mind and sets the tone for the rest of the day. Assign a time each day that feels most comfortable with your routine. Clear your mind, relax, and embrace this calm moment to be with the Lord. When you do, God promises in His Word that a person who "dwells in the secret place of the Most High shall remain stable" (Psalm 91:1 AMPC). Here's your answer to emotional stability. Connect with God, invest time with Him, listen for His voice.

> One single word can shape you, stretch you, and provide the direction you need for an entire year.

God desires private time with you. Go somewhere quiet where no one can bother you, and give your heavenly Father your full attention.

Behind-the-Scenes Habits
That Drive Crazy Success

HABIT #1

Listen up for what God is speaking to your heart by scheduling time to be alone, to think and journal. It's the alone advantage that leads to discovering God's will for your life.

> But when you pray, go into your most private room, close the door and pray to your Father who is in secret, and your Father who sees [what is done] in secret will reward you.
> —MATTHEW 6:6 AMP

PART 2

Clean Up!

CHAPTER 4

Your Laundry Isn't Finished

If you want to change the world, start off by making your bed.
—ADMIRAL BILL MCRAVEN (NAVY SEAL)

Back in the early 1970s when my parents were starting the journey of full-time ministry, my dad traveled nonstop and my mom stayed at home with my sister and me. My parents barely had any money and trusted God to pay every bill. Our house was about to be condemned. Our old car had over 100,000 miles on it, and my mom was wearing cut-down maternity dresses from her pregnancy with me two years earlier. They were living by faith, daily trusting God to provide.

One typical day, my mom was going about her household chores—doing laundry, cooking, cleaning, and caring for two small children. As she collected the clothes from the dryer and tossed them onto the guest room bed until time to wear something from the pile, she heard this phrase in her heart: *Finish your laundry.*

"What? What was that? Who was that?"

She heard it again, so softly in her heart: *Finish your laundry.* She heard this phrase again and again: *Finish what you start and take care of what you've got . . . and then God will bless you with better.*

God was teaching her a lesson. I like to call it the "Laundry Basket Law of Success."

The Laundry Basket Law of Success

My mom was learning to apply Matthew 25:21: "You have been faithful with a few things [the laundry]; I will put you in charge of many things [a global ministry]." The New Century Version says, "Because you were *loyal with small things*, I will let you care for *much greater things*."

In the silence with nobody watching, God was teaching my mom a powerful law of success: *excellence*. He was showing her that she had not finished the laundry when the clothes and towels were thrown on a bed and remained there until time to pull something out of the wrinkled pile to use. That wasn't *caring* for small things. That wasn't finishing what she started. She learned to iron her old maternity dresses, hang them up, wear them with dignity, and thank God for them. She learned to fold the towels and put them away until time to wrap up in them.

Then He taught her that she hadn't finished the dishes when they were left in the dishwasher until time to pull them out and eat from them again. They were finished only when they were dried and put back in the cabinet where they belonged. He taught her to establish standards of excellence with the little that she had so He could bless her with more.

God taught her in private so He could one day promote her in public. As she practiced this habit of excellence alone day after day, week after week, God began trusting her with nicer things. She began to get rid of her reshaped maternity dresses and purchased new, flattering dresses. She acquired finer towels, prettier dishes, newer carpet, and eventually drove a much nicer car and owned a bigger, nicer house. God began to prosper and promote my parents in ways they had only dreamed of as they began placing significance on finishing what they started and taking care of what they had.

Joyce Meyer has shared how God couldn't release her on the world until she got victory over a sink full of dirty dishes. She had to take care of what she had at home with nobody around before she could televise her broadcast across the globe. She goes as far as to say that God dealt with her for *years* about putting her grocery cart back in the designated spot rather than leaving it situated up against the curb in the parking lot.[1] When this finally became her routine, she was able to move on to bigger and better responsibilities.

• • •

I'll never forget when I began the habit of aloneness and journaling my time in prayer. I sat in the stillness of my home with my journal propped on the arm of my chair and my pen in my right hand. I closed my eyes and did my best to hear that still, small voice. The first directive I heard in prayer was not to write books that could impact lives or start a women's conference and call it something sweet or to support safe houses for young women. I received one clear directive that would prove to be the prerequisite for my success:

Clean up!

Yes, that was my first God-given vision for my life. To clean! I know, I wasn't thrilled about it either. In fact, I even questioned, *Is that truly the voice of God or the voice of my mom* (in my head)*?* I was unsure whether I could hear God's voice and, if I did, is that really what He would instruct me to do with my life? Disinfect. Scrub. Fold. Scour.

At a time when my life was falling apart, my marriage was barely hanging on, and I was desperate to hear from God, those words became my vision, my aim, my daily motivation. I have discovered since then why God would tell me to do something so simple.

Come to find out, there is a direct link between organization and success. I have read numerous success books that clearly advise us to clean up the clutter in our lives, and becoming a person of excellence in private is a requirement for promotion in public.

Let me continue to underscore this principle with a powerful statement that supports why this matters more than you may realize. *The way you do anything is the way you do everything.* Suzanne Evans made this phrase her philosophy and the title of her book.[2]

Did you know that before the military trains soldiers to fight in combat, they must first go through extensive training in Bed Making 101? Nobody makes a bed neater than our armed forces. Basic training doesn't have to do only with drills and weapons but also with making a bed with proper forty-five-degree hospital corners. Why is that? The enemy is not going to be impressed by the old "bounce a quarter off of the bed" trick. It is because making a bed properly instills a standard of excellence.

The way you do anything is the way you do everything.

If you're sloppy about making your bed, you'll be sloppy about loading your rifle. A cluttered environment is the sign of a cluttered mind. That's why the military gives strict attention to details in every area of training.

Imagine walking into the barracks of the United States Army and seeing mattresses with unmade beds, sheets in a pile, wadded-up blankets, and last night's clothes thrown on the floor. What kind of impression would that give you of the safety of our country? Are we in the hands of the elite or the hands of defeat?

Navy Admiral William H. McRaven, ninth commander of US Special Operations, delivered a commencement speech at the University of Texas at Austin on the ten lessons he learned during his SEAL basic training. This tough, intimidating SEAL announced to the graduates, "If you want to change the world, start off by making your bed."

Admiral McRaven was stressing the point that, as simple and unimpressive as it sounds, when you make your bed first thing in the morning, you will instantly sense a feeling of accomplishment and productivity. And in doing so, it will inspire you to tackle "another task and another and another."[3]

It's not just about housekeeping; it's about your personal standard. Your level of respect for yourself and your family shows up in your surroundings. Excellence is simply doing ordinary, everyday, mundane tasks behind the scenes in an extraordinary way.

To be honest, my directive from the Lord sounded futile, knowing how far I needed to go in my life. This instruction came at a time when I was blatantly miserable. As I mentioned, I was confused, hurt, unhappy, and in dire need of vision.

I didn't have a success coach come to my house and lay out a growth track for me to follow. I didn't have a mentor to lead me in a strategic plan. I didn't have a simple book telling me that decluttering could transform my mental health, my energy, and my relationships, and set me on a career path that would boggle my mind. I didn't even have an indication of what God wanted me to do with my life. All I knew was that I heard those simple words, *clean up*, and that became all the direction I needed for that season of my life.

I took those words literally and seriously. I began with one room, one section at a time, starting with the kitchen. In addition to my cleaning products—my broom, my mop, and my latex gloves—I carried one vitally important "cleaning" item: a CD player loaded with faith-building audios. I wanted to renew my mind of all the painful thoughts I was entertaining, restore my focus, and rebuild my faith. Since "faith comes from hearing" (Romans 10:17), I was doing the cleaning on the outside but God was cleaning me on the inside.

With the kitchen being my first vision, I set the timer for twenty minutes, and I stayed focused on that room alone. As I carried items from the kitchen that belonged in other rooms of the house, my tendency would be to start cleaning that other disorganized space. But I had to say, "No, Terri, stay focused on one room alone until it is finished with excellence."

I transferred the stack of bills strewn across the kitchen desk to a designated drawer in the office. I hung the car keys on a hook in the laundry room. I took the jogging shoes from the kitchen floor next to the table and put them away in the closet where they belonged. I hung the jackets in the coat closet instead of leaving them draped over a kitchen chair. I loaded the dishwasher. I cleaned off the countertops. I emptied out the refrigerator filled with expired food and take-out boxes. I sprayed, scrubbed, and wiped down every square inch of the stubborn ketchup spills and strawberry leaks in the bottom of the refrigerator drawers.

I was on a mission! I was energized by each section of cleanliness. I was disgusted by the disarray. I was motivated by vision. And I was being transformed by the Word of God in the process. Every square inch of the kitchen was clean and in order. The floors were mopped, the appliances were wiped down, the counters were cleared, the window blinds were opened, and a candle was lit. I felt such a sense of confidence. I was pleased and proud to visibly see my progress. It brought such peace into my home and into my mind.

Getting my kitchen in order did more for me mentally than it did physically. I felt charged up. Although my circumstances were still a huge mess, I had order in this area of my life and that gave me serenity. Once that tedious but profitable process was complete, it was time to move on to room number two: my bedroom.

Again I carried my little CD player and pushed Play.

After every single room, closet, drawer, and cabinet in my entire home was what I would define as clean and excellent, I had more peace than ever before. I had done so much in private that nobody knew about but me and God.

I never dreamed that exactly nine months after receiving that instruction to clean up, I would be promoted to CEO of an international organization overseeing eight offices around the world! God was truly preparing me for promotion. He was observing how I could manage small things in order to lead greater things.

You might be questioning, "Terri, you couldn't become a senior vice president until you got your sock drawer organized?" Our handbook for life says, "If you are faithful in *little* things, you will be faithful in *large* ones. But if you are dishonest in little things, you won't be honest with greater responsibilities" (Luke 16:10 NLT). The NIV translation says, "Whoever can be trusted with very little can also be trusted with much."

Your personal standard of excellence is all about preparation for something greater. On a podcast I once heard a minister say, "What's *next* in your life is always connected to what's *now.*" God is watching, observing, and noticing how you care for the little things in your life behind closed doors.

The Bible says that Daniel became distinguished above all other high officials because "an *excellent spirit* was in him" (Daniel 6:3 KJV). His personal standard of excellence brought him to one of the highest positions in his society. He wasn't just your average Joe working an average job. He was one of the foreigners in exile brought by the king to "indoctrinate them in the Babylonian language and the lore of magic and fortunetelling" (Daniel 1:3–5 MSG). But God's favor was on him, and Daniel was promoted to one of three administrators who supervised the entire kingdom.

Scripture says, "Daniel was *preferred* above the presidents and princes" (Daniel 6:3 KJV). The word *preferred* means to be hand-picked, approved, adopted, liked, and endorsed.[4] He was promoted in public for what he practiced in private.

Your standard of excellence can pave the way for you to be promoted when you seem to be the least likely, the last choice, the shock of the season to those around you. It will cause you to be set apart and promoted above others who may be more qualified, educated, and experienced than you are! Excellence in private opens doors in your life in public. Excellence puts you on a path for success.

Think about it: If I couldn't get my house in order, how could I get an organization in order? If I was a mess, my leadership would be a mess. I had to adopt a standard of excellence before I could expect excellence from my team. God was preparing me in private for a major promotion in public.

The way you do anything is the way you do everything.

CHAPTER 5

10 Reasons Successful People Are Organized

Let all things be done decently and in order.
—1 CORINTHIANS 14:40 KJV

Julie Harvey shares a fun anecdote of how her organizational skills helped her in renting a home. She was meeting the landlord at the location to view the property, and the landlord greeted her at her car instead of at the house. Julie was surprised when the landlord began asking her detailed questions about her car, a Honda Accord. After they'd discussed how long Julie had owned it and what she thought about it, the landlord led her inside to view the rental house.

After touring the home, Julie knew she wanted to rent it and asked the landlord if there'd been much interest from other potential renters. The reply was confusing: "Yes, I have shown this place to several people, but quite honestly, you are the only person I would consider renting it to."

They signed a lease immediately, because the landlord had decided that only someone who took proper care of their car would be sure to take proper care of a house.[1]

The level of your organization or disorganization says a lot about you and the opportunities available to you. Your outer world reflects your inner world.

Getting organized is consistently one of the top five New Year's resolutions, but 84 percent of people say at any given time their house is a mess![2] If most people fail in decluttering and getting organized, then why even put forth all this effort? We've seen the significance of orderliness from God's Word, but let's look at ten practical benefits of being organized.

1. You'll save money. Instead of buying things you already have (AA batteries, soap, glue, scissors, socks, lightbulbs, cleaning supplies, and so forth), you will know exactly where to locate them and save money you don't need to spend.

Disorganization is a drain on your wallet. You'll eliminate excess money flying out the door by having your bills organized properly, which will ensure they are always paid on time.

2. You can find things. Have you lost your keys or your cell phone *again*? The *New Yorker* shared that the average American spends six months of their lives looking for lost or misplaced items.[3] What could you do with an extra six months added to your life? Seriously consider what clutter and chaos are costing you. Think of the progress you could make writing that book, launching that ministry, starting that business, getting that degree, learning that second language, traveling the world, volunteering at that safe house when instead you're searching for the remote control for six months!

3. You'll save time. Pixie's "Lost & Found" survey found that Americans spend "2.5 days a year looking for misplaced items."[4] That's nearly an hour a week wasted.

4. You can be more creative. Having an orderly, clean space allows your mind to relax and be more focused and productive. When your area is in shape, your brain doesn't have to work

> Having an orderly, clean space allows your mind to relax and be more focused and productive.

so hard. Your mind is sharp, your concentration is focused, and the order around you feels good.

5. Your life will be less stressed. Your mood is affected by your surroundings. Sixty-three percent of surveyed Americans said that organizing helped reduce their stress levels.[5] Scientific studies have linked clutter and disorganization to depression and anxiety.[6]

Organizing experts have reported their clients have lost weight, ended toxic relationships, left unhealthy jobs, and stopped bad habits once they decluttered their lives. Clearing your space clears up your mind as well.

6. You'll sleep better. We spend one-third of our lives in the bedroom, which is more time than in any other room in the house. This room is designed for rest, relaxation, and sleep. Studies show that people with clutter in their bedrooms experience more sleep disturbances.[7]

There's nothing more peaceful than climbing into bed with clean sheets and warm blankets, and then drifting off to sleep in a tidy bedroom. Imagine the floors vacuumed or mopped, the clothes folded in the dresser, the nightstand cleared of clutter, and the soft aroma of fresh lavender calming your mind and senses.

7. You'll have more time and energy to go after your dreams and goals. When your home is dirty or disorganized, it's difficult to focus on bigger tasks. When you're not always feeling the pressure of needing to get that room cleaned up, you can focus your time and energy on the bigger goals of life rather than the maintenance of life. Your mind is free to plan other things.

8. You'll be a great example for your family. Your children and family are watching, observing, and learning from you every day. Showing them how to keep things clutter-free and organized will help prepare them for success. An orderly home reduces stress, anxiety, and chaos.

9. You'll build better relationships. It is embarrassing to have unexpected guests show up when your house is messy and

disorganized. When this repeatedly happens, you tend to not invite anyone over. Don't allow a messy home to prevent you from spending time with the people you love.

Your home does not have to be in museum-like form to be presentable or host your best friends, but keeping things clean and clutter-free can be managed.

10. You'll have more confidence. Clutter has a strong effect on moods and overall self-esteem.[8] Women, especially, feel embarrassed, ashamed, and guilty with the presence of clutter.

When you organize your home (to your personal standard), you will feel more competent, in control, and empowered. Getting your house in shape will improve your self-esteem and self-image. You will develop confidence in your "castle." Your home truly becomes your haven.

As you can see, the little inconveniences of cleaning are worth it in the long run when they produce a checklist of benefits causing you to feel happier, healthier, and possibly even wealthier.

CHAPTER 6

Get Your 20-Minute Timer

Closets can be a window into people's mental health.
—MELINDA BECK

When I was a little girl, my dad pastored a church in Fort Worth, Texas. There was a family attending the church who had a dream of owning a brand-new Cadillac. This particular family was clear on their vision, and they continually told my dad, "We are declaring that we have a brand-new Cadillac, debt-free, in Jesus' name!"

One day my dad said, "Let me see the car you're currently driving." They walked him out to the parking lot. With one glance, anyone could see why they were not driving a brand-new Cadillac debt-free, no matter how clear the vision was or how consistent their declarations were. Their car was filthy. It looked like something from a junkyard.

My dad said, "God is not going to bless you with a better car when you don't take care of the car you've got." Then he shared a secret to success. He said, "*Act as if* this car were the Cadillac. Show God that you can be trusted with a nicer vehicle. If you don't take care of this car, give it a few months—your new Cadillac would look just like this!" I hate to say that I never saw them acquire that new Cadillac, but I also never saw them clean up their car.

God won't bless us with *more* when we are not faithful with *little*. If you're believing God for a new car, a new job, a new house,

Practice excellence now on the way to where you desire to be.

a new ministry, or a new career, one of the greatest strategies for success is to *act as if* you already have what you want to have. Practice excellence now on the way to where you desire to be.

Excellence is one of God's character traits. Genesis 1:31 says, "God saw all that he had made, and it was very good." Notice it doesn't say, "God saw all that He had made, and it was *average*." Or "God saw all that He had made and it was *acceptable* (or *mediocre*)." No, it was *very good*.

As you go about your day today, look at your surroundings: your work, your home, your pantry, your closet, your car, your endeavors. Can you say it is very good?

Your outer world reflects your inner world. Brian Tracy said,

> The car you drive and the condition that you keep it in will correspond to your state of mind at any given time. When you are feeling positive and confident and in control of your life, your home, your car and your workplace will tend to be well-organized and efficient. When you feel overwhelmed with work, or frustrated and unhappy, your car, your workplace, your home, even your closets will tend to reflect this state of disarray and confusion. . . . Everything is from the inner to the outer.[1]

Psychologists believe that our homes mirror our emotional state.[2] If your items are always lost, perhaps you feel lost in life. If your house feels out of control, perhaps your life feels out of control. If you're always overwhelmed with how much to clean, perhaps you're overwhelmed by your to-do list.

In an article titled "Why Clutter Matters and Decluttering Is Difficult," Amanda Enayati tells the eye-opening story of pouring her heart out to professional organizer Jennifer Hunter. Amanda told her, "I feel like if I could just get rid of all this clutter, I could go on to do great things."

Hunter immediately replied, "Maybe that's why you keep the clutter."

Amanda felt defensive. Surely, she wasn't insinuating that her disorganization and clutter represented some sort of internal permission for underachievement! Or maybe it did.[3]

Remember, there is a direct link between organization and success. The organization of your surroundings reflects the organization of your life. To put it mildly, *clutter blocks success*. When there's clutter in your home, there will be a degree of clutter in you.

Comfort and Clutter Do Not Go Hand in Hand

Keep in mind that everyone's idea of a clean, clutter-free, and organized home will be different. Don't feel guilty about what you decide is best for you. The goal is to create order, tranquility, and new behavior patterns behind the scenes that lead you to a more productive, rewarding life in public.

Are you ready to start decluttering, getting organized, and preparing for your promotion? Follow this checklist as a guideline:

Write the Vision

Before you get started, plan. Take a walk through your home and write the general vision for each room. Then focus on one room and begin making a list of *every single thing* that needs to be done in that room. A few examples:

Kitchen

- Load dishwasher
- Take mail to proper place
- Remove everything on countertops
- Clean microwave
- Clean out refrigerator
- Clean oven
- Sweep and mop floors

Master Bedroom

- Put shoes in closet
- Trash newspapers
- Remove pile of books
- Clean off nightstand
- Vacuum floor

Believe me, tackling one room and making it a masterpiece will give you such a boost of confidence that you will be motivated to go after the other rooms with gusto!

Start with One Room

How do you know which room to start decluttering and organizing? It's simple. Start with the room you spend the most time in. You need a constant reminder of completion and accomplishment, so attack that room first. Choose one that doesn't contain a great deal of sentimental items so you can make great progress at the outset. It could be the kitchen, if that's where the family seems to congregate the most—eating meals, doing homework, and visiting. The best room to start with will differ from person to person.

Start with What's Visible

Before you begin cleaning out the refrigerator, the kitchen pantry, or the spice rack, always tackle the clutter that can be seen. You need to see your progress immediately to stay motivated to keep going. If you decided to start your organizing in the kitchen area, begin by loading the dishes piled up in the sink. Place all food left on the counter back in the pantry or refrigerator. Wipe off the countertops. Place the pile of bills in the home office or on the kitchen desk. Take the shoes to the closet and the newspapers to the trash.

Push Play

This is a vital piece in the cleanup challenge. You need to intentionally fill yourself up with positive input. Whoever has your ear has your life. Find your favorite inspirational YouTube channels or podcasts or download an audiobook (perhaps this one), and push Play. Trust me when I say that this is equally as important as cleaning the physical clutter on the outside, because God will be cleansing the mental and emotional clutter on the inside.

You will be amazed how much your mood is affected by what you're hearing. Just a little dose of hearing faith-building messages will defeat depression, eliminate anxiety, and inspire you to believe God for impossible dreams. Your mindset will be elevated as a result of what your ears are hearing. My pastor Keith Craft says, "When you elevate your thinking, you'll elevate your life."

This simple act of listening to something faith-building, motivational, and instructional each time I clean not only gives me a strong foundation in God's Word but also leads to learning everything from time management to leadership skills, financial planning, fitness tips, and even brushing up on my French. You can drastically change the direction of your life by changing what you're feeding your mind.

> Hearing faith-building messages will defeat depression, eliminate anxiety, and inspire you to believe God for impossible dreams.

Set Your Timer for Twenty Minutes and Go Full Speed Ahead

You will be amazed at what you can accomplish with a twenty-minute plan. It is more motivating to set aside small sessions of time to declutter than trying to attack it all at once. So I always recommend setting your timer for twenty minutes and just getting started. If you can allot more time, two or three hours at most, then set a goal to see how much you can accomplish by focusing on one room.

We tend to put off decluttering and organizing because we think it will demand an entire day, and I realize that some areas do require a chunk of time, but I am always amazed at how much can be accomplished within a short time frame. Twenty minutes a day over the course of a month is ten hours of getting your home in shape!

For example, not too long ago I dreaded opening my makeup drawer each morning because of how much junk had accumulated. Old eye shadow palettes, dried-up mascara tubes, outdated lip liners, and so on. I kept thinking, *When I have a day at home, I'm going to tackle this drawer.* It's rare that I have a full day at home, so I finally set aside twenty minutes to work on the drawer and see how far I could go. It took only twelve minutes!

As I was decluttering and organizing one day, I heard John Maxwell make this bold claim that altered my entire life.

If I could come to your house and spend just one day with you, I would be able to tell whether or not you will be successful. You could pick the day. If I got up with you in the morning and went through the day with you, watching you for twenty-four hours, I could tell in what direction your life is headed. . . . You will never change your life until you change something you do *daily*. You see, success doesn't just suddenly occur one day in someone's life. For that matter, neither does failure. Each is a process. Every day of your life is merely preparation for the next. What you become is the result of what you do today.[4]

That philosophy changed the entire trajectory of my life.

This book is not to brag on my accomplishments or to take credit for the favor of God on my life. I don't want to imply that I've got it all together and my life is a piece of cake (or cupcake)! The truth is that I've had my share of struggles, disappointments, and heartbreak; however, my story is one of hope for what is possible with a simple change in your routine behind the scenes.

Behind-the-Scenes Habits
That Drive Crazy Success

HABIT #2

Clean up by starting with one room, one section, one twenty-minute chunk at a time. It's the alone advantage that leads to getting your life in order.

Whatever you do, do all to the glory of God.
—1 CORINTHIANS 10:31 NKJV

PART 3

Wake Up!

CHAPTER 7

You Can Conquer the Covers

Success is the sum of small efforts, repeated day in and day out.
—ASCRIBED TO ROBERT COLLIER

My father, Jerry Savelle, felt called into the ministry in 1969. He knew he needed to prepare as much as possible to deliver sermons that could impact lives. That would include reading the Bible and studying it intensely.

At the time he was undisciplined about getting up early, but he had to start investing in himself if he was going to pursue his big dream! He set the alarm for six o'clock the next morning. The alarm sounded, and he immediately got up, full of determination. He walked into the guest bedroom, lay across the bed with his Bible open, and began reading. An hour later, he woke up.

This routine repeated itself day after day until he got so frustrated that he realized the bed was too tempting; he needed to sit up in a chair. Unfortunately, the chair was equally as cozy and rocked him right to sleep.

One day my father came across a familiar scripture: "If you continue in My word, then you are truly my disciples [disciplined ones]; and you will know the truth, and the truth will set you free" (John 8:31–32 NASB). Although he had read that verse many times before, this time the word *continue* stood out as the biggest word on the page.

He thought, *That's my problem! I quit everything. I quit college. I quit working at the Chevrolet dealership. I quit working at the Ford dealership. I quit the Mercury dealership. When things don't go my way, I quit. I've never "continued" anything.*

In that moment, he began the journey of continuing by disciplining himself.

Desperate for change in his life and his habits, he was so determined to continue that he walked into his bathroom early one morning and stood on the edge of the bathtub, literally balancing himself and holding his Bible in the palms of his hands, saying, "Jerry Savelle, you better not fall asleep or you're gonna bust your head! You better *continue!*"

That was the beginning of a lifetime of discipline conquering the covers.

Conquering the Covers

This comical but life-changing story of desperation worked! My dad is one of the most disciplined people I know. His resolute decision to change his habits has resulted in establishing offices all over the world, airing a television broadcast in more than two hundred nations, authoring more than seventy books, and ministering in thousands of churches in nations across the globe *because he conquered the covers*!

When most people hear success stories, they see only how the person looks after they're successful. It's easy to get inspired by their achievements, and it's great to get motivated, but if you really want to learn from someone's success, you need to learn what they did behind the scenes to get there. You need to know what they're doing in private that promoted them in public. They're balancing on bathtubs!

Until 2002 I didn't realize that each morning I lost the "battle of the bed" it was taking me further from success. Each morning that I slept an extra thirty minutes was compounding to an extra fifteen hours each month that could change my life or keep me stuck.

The most successful people in the world have something in common: they practice *mind over mattress*. They conquer the covers! From political leaders and ministers to famous athletes, CEOs, and celebrities, they cherish the morning hours to get up and invest in themselves while the rest of the world chooses to snooze.

Benjamin Franklin said, "Early to bed and early to rise makes a man healthy, wealthy, and wise."[1] More than two hundred years later, early risers are still among the most productive, wealthy, and successful people. Waking up early enables you to take control of your day first thing in the morning rather than the day controlling you.

In desperate need of change in my life, I decided to take control of my morning routine. And what I thought would be a simple change on the hands of the clock turned into a drastic change to the discipline in my life. Just going to bed a little earlier, so I could wake up a little earlier, made me feel more in control of my day and my life. Instead of waking up feeling scattered, rushed, and everything last minute, I started waking up and giving myself plenty of time to feel prepared for the day.

You've heard the quote, "You can't pour from an empty cup." You must fill yourself up first so you're able to pour out to others.

Bestselling author Jon Acuff explained this empty cup principle by sharing how the only way he could be consistent in his personal growth (in addition to working a full-time job and raising a family with his wife) was to start "being selfish at 5 a.m." He began the discipline of getting up at the crack of dawn to read, to listen to messages, to journal, to write, to pray. He reported that since he began this early morning ritual, "Not one time has my wife complained that I wasn't spending time with her at 5 a.m. Not one time has my daughter asked me to ride bikes with her at 5 a.m., nor has my other daughter asked me to jump rope." He said, "That's *your* time to focus on you, your personal development. . . . Own your mornings!"[2]

If the idea of setting your alarm thirty minutes earlier sounds horrible, then you may not be ready to get out of a rut, to go above average, and to live your dreams. I've heard this quote attributed to Jon Acuff: "If your dream isn't worth thirty minutes, you've either got the wrong dream or you're just pretending you have one."

And that's the realization I had to come to if I was going to change my life. In fact, I heard someone define the word *P.O.O.R.* as Passing Over Opportunities Repeatedly. You might say, "But, Terri, that's just it. I haven't had any opportunities." My argument is this: Yes, you have. Every morning at five (or six or seven), with nobody watching but you and God, you have another opportunity to get up and invest in your future.

Legendary motivator Zig Ziglar encouraged goal-oriented people to replace the term *alarm clock*, which is negative, with the term *opportunity clock*, which is positive. Immediately, when the opportunity clock goes off, your mind is headed in a positive direction about what the day will bring![3]

You don't have to get up before sunrise, but those who consistently wake up early are more productive than those who sleep late. Start this new routine by setting your alarm twenty or thirty minutes earlier than normal (but also go to bed earlier than usual). Morning rituals can change your life and lead you to success.

Take an inventory of your current routine. You already have one, but the question is, Does it support your goals? Is it helping you get closer to where you want to be? Are you waking up with determination and, even better, going to sleep with satisfaction that you seized the last twenty-four hours? Or are you in that place I was in for eleven years—waking up frantic, rushing, dashing out the door hoping you haven't forgotten anything, and going to sleep feeling dissatisfied with all the to-dos left undone on the list?

Leave the Familiar

Here's what you need to know about your mind: the brain loves what's familiar. Ninety-seven percent of diets fail[4] year after year, probably in part because of the unfamiliar. I heard a therapist on YouTube say that your brain rejects new things and always wants to go back to what it recognizes. For example, if you always eat a bowl of cereal for breakfast and now you're trying a diet that says to eat one hard-boiled egg every morning, your brain will work hard to reject this new habit and go back to what's familiar, the cereal.

When you first start waking up earlier, in the beginning you may dread it, and your brain will fight for the right to keep you in bed. But the good news is you can make anything familiar.

For example, for years I was addicted to drinking sweet tea every single day. The habit started when one of my friends told me Chicken Express had forty-nine-cent, extra-large sweet teas! I tasted one and it was delicious. I ordered one the next day and the next day. It was so convenient to drive by on my way home, get that jumbo iced tea, and hey, it's pocket change—two quarters! The next thing you know, my car was on autopilot after work every day, as I craved those gigantic Styrofoam cups full of sugar. Some people even started calling me "Sweet T" (Terri).

What happened? My brain started recognizing that this behavior was my new normal, so I subconsciously added a new habit to my life. Finally, I decided it was time to break the sweet tea addiction. It wasn't easy. I had to decide on a new familiar. I remember forcing myself to drink water—plain, clear, boring water. My body screamed for that sugary sweet tea. I remember eating pizza with the family one night and thinking, *You can't have pizza with water.* But I forced myself to drink one bottle of water. I did it the next day and the next day and the next day. Little by little water became my new familiar habit. More than twenty years later, I don't crave sweet tea.

You can make anything familiar by doing it repeatedly.

I found out that the number one way to build your confidence, your self-esteem, and your new identity of discipline boils down to this: building a reputation with yourself. What kind of reputation? A history of keeping the promises you make to you.

Once you know you can keep your word with a few simple things, like waking up earlier, it builds your reputation with yourself; it builds momentum, and that builds your faith! When you've successfully kept your word to yourself for three weeks, you begin to confidently think, *What else can I do? I'm a goal-setting machine!*

When we look at other people, many times we see the glory but we don't see the story. In 2002 I had to decide to not be like a plastic bag in the middle of a parking lot, floating around with every gust of wind. I had to get focused on my new identity—my new reputation with myself first—before anyone else noticed it. I didn't tell a soul what I was doing. I had to learn to keep my promises to me of waking up a little bit earlier than I was used to. Once I established my reputation with myself, others noticed. As the saying goes, your repetition is your reputation.

Honestly, if someone like me, who formerly slept until the last minute for eleven years, can now eagerly get up at the crack of dawn for more than twenty years, then you can too. I heard Jim Rohn give this memorable analogy about a goose. He said the goose operates by two things: instinct and the genetic code.

For example, the goose flies south every year. "How often?" you ask. Every winter. Even if you told the goose, "Hey, it would be best to fly west this year," he ignores that advice because he can't make decisions on his own. He can only operate by instinct and the genetic code. But here's the mic drop: not human beings. We can live a certain way for ten years, twenty years, forty years, and then one day, decide to tear up the script and live a completely different life. Jim Rohn said, "Write this down: *you're not a goose!*"[5]

You can change your life any time you decide to. And that change begins by setting your alarm twenty minutes, thirty minutes, one hour earlier.

Let's discover what successful people are doing before sunrise.

CHAPTER 8

5 Things Successful People Do Before Breakfast

Before anything else, preparation is the key to success.
—ALEXANDER GRAHAM BELL

I heard a story about a success coach who met with the Atlanta Falcons football team for a motivational pep talk. He instructed these big guys to get out a sheet of paper and write down their biggest dreams. One by one, they followed his advice. After the first assignment was complete, he asked them to hold their written aspirations up in the air. They complied.

With their arms lifted high, showing they were full of big dreams, he said, "Now rip them up!"

"These guys were not happy about this experiment—at all!" the coach recalled. Reluctantly, and with nostrils flaring, they submitted to the nonsense.

The coach finally asked, "How many other players have the exact dream you have? To win a championship? To win a conference? To go to the Super Bowl? To win the Super Bowl? Everyone in the NFL has these goals. Are the goals alone going to get you to where you want to go? No. Not by themselves. Now write down your *commitments* to achieve the goals."

Wow! What will *you* commit to each day that will lead you to your greatest dreams?

As you've followed along my journey from 2002 until today, you recall the former miserable person I was—on the verge of a divorce, lonely, insecure, visionless, and merely surviving—until I started waking myself up earlier. I made a list of five things I would practice every day for twenty-one days: pray and meditate, read, listen to audio teaching, write down dreams and goals, and exercise.

Endeavoring to start new habits in my life, I was determined to stick with these disciplines for three solid weeks with no exception. I never dreamed that twenty-four years later, I would still be practicing these five life-changing habits.

1. Pray and Meditate

Michael Todd, author of *Crazy Faith*, wrote, "Make seeking God a part of your regular routine now in private so that one day you'll be ready to do what God asks you to do in front of an audience."[1]

An interesting story that supports this comes from Robert J. Morgan: "When the president of the United States arrives in the West Wing each morning, the Presidential Daily Briefing is lying on the Oval Office desk. The PDB is usually about fifteen pages long and is accompanied by a visit from a high-ranking official . . . who provides face-to-face insights."[2] Apparently, they have been practicing this procedure since the Truman presidency.

"When George W. Bush was elected to the White House, his father, former president George H. W. Bush, told him to never miss these top-of-the-morning meetings, for they are the most important part of the president's day."[3]

Hearing the presidents' routine makes me think that's exactly how we should feel about our appointment with God. The time is flexible; the habit isn't. Although we've already discussed the importance of setting time aside to be alone, to pray, and to journal, make it a priority to never miss your top-of-the-morning appointment to pray.

. . .

Hall-of-fame athletes, red-carpet actors, platinum-recording artists, and global leaders all meditate. No matter what religion they are affiliated with, successful people make prayer or meditation a top priority in their day. People from all faiths, backgrounds, and careers have discovered this success habit helps them relax, unwind, and improve their personal lives.

The late Kobe Bryant said, "I meditate every day. It's like having an anchor. If I don't do it, I feel like I'm constantly chasing the day as opposed to being in control and dictating my day. I have a calmness about whatever comes my way, a poise, and that comes from starting my morning off with meditation."[4]

I have read numerous articles and books sharing information about the rich, the famous, and the most successful, who all commit to some form of daily meditation. Examples include actors (Jennifer Aniston, Tom Hanks, Hugh Jackman), supermodels (Gisele Bundchen), recording artists (Sheryl Crow and Katy Perry), comedians (Jerry Seinfeld), and authors (Jack Canfield and Tony Robbins).[5]

I am not endorsing all types of meditation. I'm simply pointing out that prayer and meditation on God's Word is a solution for success prescribed by God Himself. Some recommend focusing on the universe; however, I communicate with the Creator of the universe. I am only endorsing prayer and meditation with the one true God and His Word, the Holy Bible, which is our manual for success.

When we meditate as Christians, we reflect on God's Word and we listen for Him. Prayer is you talking to God; meditation is you listening for God. Many times, we wonder if He will speak to us. His Word says, "My sheep listen to my voice" (John 10:27). When you sit quietly in His presence, listen for that still, small voice on the inside of you, and get into a habit of just writing down whatever you hear.

Through meditating, you will discover more focus, direction, and wisdom for your life than through any other habit.

This single habit of prayer and meditation is the forerunner for all others. It is the one you need more than any other habit. If you just incorporate this one, primary change in your routine, it will dramatically affect everything in your life.

2. Read (A Lot!)

W. Clement Stone, the former publisher of *Success Magazine* who was worth $800 million, began to mentor young Jack Canfield in the early 1970s. During an interview with him, Stone wanted to get an idea of how much Canfield valued personal development.

He asked, "I have a question for you. Do you watch television?"

Canfield replied, "Yes, of course."

Stone asked, "How many hours a day do you watch TV?"

"I don't know. I watch shows like *Good Morning America*. The news. Johnny Carson. Maybe about three hours a day."

"Cut out one hour a day," said Stone.

"Okay. But why?"

"If you cut out that one hour per day and you multiply that by 365 days in a year, that's 365 hours. Divide that by a forty-hour workweek and you now have nine-and-a-half weeks of productive time," said Stone. "I want that time."

"What do you want me to do?" asked Canfield.

"I want you to *read*! Read anything in your field that will help you. Read stories. Read psychology. Read management. Read about marketing. Read about this arena that we play the game in," said Stone. "If you do this, you will not only become more valuable to me, but to yourself."

Jack Canfield took Mr. Stone's life-changing advice to heart by establishing a routine of reading a simple dose every day. Consequently, Canfield has gone down in the Guinness World Records for writing and selling the most number one bestselling books at the same time from his classic *Chicken Soup for the Soul* series.[6] What if he'd continued to watch that extra hour of TV each night?

Success is tied to your personal development. You can't grow more if you don't learn more. I heard that Dan Lier was once asked what he considered to be the number one key to being successful. He answered, "Consistency. If it's not a habit or a hobby it won't get done. The key is to make it a habit."

I hated reading in the beginning. I had to force myself because in my mind reading was always an obligation, not an opportunity. But I found out that if I truly wanted my life to grow, I had to make it a habit. Morning after morning and week after week, I read in private with nobody watching. But as I began to grow, everything began to grow.

3. Listen to Audio Teaching

This is the easiest of all the habits to adopt. It only requires two words and very little physical effort: *push Play!* As we just discovered, successful people read each morning, but they also take advantage of other available means to increase their knowledge by listening to audio teaching. Whether that's during their jog or weightlifting routine, during their commute to the office, or as they scrub down the refrigerator, they grow as they go.

Find messages from ministers who speak faith, hope, encouragement, inspiration, and truth from the Word of God and listen to them intentionally. Instead of having the television on in the background while you cook, listen to a message that ignites your spirit to dream bigger. Every time you do, faith comes!

Each time faith is deposited into your spirit, you begin to think differently, you start dreaming bigger, your confidence grows, your fears subside, and you more truly believe that all things are possible with God. As Zig Ziglar has said, "Your input shapes your outlook, and your outlook shapes your outcome."

When I first began, in 2002, listening to teaching while decluttering and organizing my house, my goal was to also listen each morning as part of my ritual while getting ready for the day. *I've got to get ready anyway; I might as well learn something.* And having *The Price Is Right* on in the background wasn't going to improve my life.

Next I found a pink sticky note, scribbled down the words *push Play*, and stuck it to my mirror. Because my previous routine was to listen to music to get my blood flowing in the morning, I needed this pink reminder staring me in the face when I looked up from brushing my teeth.

I'll never forget that first morning when I glanced at the command and thought, *Oh yeah, push Play.* And the routine began. I did it again the next day and the next and the next, until I could remove the message on the mirror because pushing Play had become a habit. To this day, I press the little button. And I can't even put a price on what I've learned each morning while I'm simply gluing on my eyelashes.

4. Write (and Review) Dreams and Goals

Writing your dreams and goals is a clear key to success!

Everyone seems to agree on the importance of writing down goals. A recent study at Dominican University confirmed that "those who wrote their goals accomplished significantly more than those who did not write their goals."[7] The very act of penning your aspirations on paper is a very powerful motivator. It forces you to get specific about your ambitions. Tony Robbins said, "Setting goals is the first step in turning the invisible into the visible."[8] (I'll explain this success habit in detail in part 5.)

I once read about how actress Emma Stone went against all odds to pursue her dream of acting by writing and creating a vision for her parents to see. She had to get crystal clear and convince them that moving to Hollywood was the best thing for their family so she could become a star. How? She not only wrote down her dream but also created an entire PowerPoint presentation.

Stone went all out in her goal of explaining why she needed to pursue a career in acting, naming her presentation "Project Hollywood." She even added background music to her proposal by playing Madonna's single "Hollywood." How could any parent refuse such a creative and well-thought-out proposition? Ultimately Stone's mother moved to Hollywood with her, since she was only fifteen years old at the time. Today Emma Stone is an Academy Award–winning actress.[9] That's the power of having your dreams and goals in writing.

5. Exercise

In high school and college I was disciplined in exercising, but doing so became more sporadic through the years. I'd start a workout program and be well disciplined when I had a big goal in front of me such as summer vacation. I'd be consistent about walking every day for a solid hour, lose the weight I wanted to lose, go on vacation, and then not work out again for nine months.

When my life hit that all-time low, I was desperate for major changes in every area. I discovered from my reading and listening that there is a link between physical health and emotional health. Just a simple walk outside in the fresh air can bring a series of health benefits and improve your overall well-being. And I needed a complete overhaul! Numerous studies have discovered that exercise is one of the most important habits you can develop. And you don't need to invest a lot of time to see the benefits. So I was determined to go all in with this new discipline.

I remember that first morning the alarm sounded at 4:45, I pushed snooze. Then fifteen minutes later I got up, slipped on my jogging shoes, added a little mascara (I just have to!), and went outside in the pitch dark. At first I was a little creeped out by the darkness in my neighborhood at that hour. Even with the streetlights still on, I could barely see my hand in front of my face. With my cell phone in my pocket and a can of pepper spray in my right hand, I began walking toward the stop sign at the end of my long street.

It was so quiet I could almost hear my own thoughts. There weren't any kids playing, cars starting up, or birds chirping; it was just me on a lonely, quiet, dark street in Crowley, Texas, with nothing to look at but the stars above me. Soon my walk went from feeling a little creepy to being incredibly peaceful. As I rounded the end of the street and headed back toward my house to conclude lap number one, I began praying silently—not out loud in case another walker was behind me and would think I was nuts.

I began talking to the Lord about what was on my heart, the pain I was feeling, the confusion I was experiencing, the mess I was in. I told Him everything. I held nothing back. I mean, He already knew, but it felt so good getting it all out. Somehow, even though I couldn't hear Him responding to me like my best friend, Theresa, does, I knew He was intently listening. The more I talked, the more I forgot how many laps I had done. Before I knew it, my alarm went off. I'd been walking and talking with the Lord for one full hour. It felt like fifteen minutes. I had to go inside and start getting my daughter ready for school, but I could hardly wait for another appointment with my best friend the next day.

I eagerly crossed off day number one of exercise on my wall

calendar. I did it the next day and the next. What I thought would be a massive chore or drudgery to keep my commitment became what I most looked forward to each day. I could hardly wait to get up and start my day with another "therapy session." At the end of twenty-one days, I couldn't imagine stopping this counseling appointment. I was gaining clarity about my life, my personality, my weaknesses, and my insecurities—all from a simple commitment to walk up and down my street each day before the sun rose. It may take you only twenty-one days to form a habit, as it did me, but James Clear says recent research reveals that "on average, it takes more than two months before a new behavior becomes automatic—sixty-six days to be exact."[10] So please don't be discouraged if it takes you longer. Bottom line, forming habits is a process.

My daily walk with the Lord opened up a whole new world to me. I drew closer to Him than I'd been in my entire life. Once you develop an intimate relationship with God, you will never be the same. If you have battled with insecurity and inferiority like I have, you will develop confidence you never knew existed. You will be free from timidity, fear, low self-esteem, passivity, and rejection. You will be free from all the debilitating mindsets that are keeping you from fulfilling your assignment on earth! God will become your best friend, your confidant, the One to whom you talk about everything.

Walking with God in your own personal way doesn't happen overnight. You don't get to know God by one life-changing encounter. It happens through relationship. We all know that relationships are built over time. The same applies to God. You have to invest yourself, your time, and your priorities into being with Him.

> You have to invest yourself, your time, and your priorities into being with God.

"Come close to God [with a contrite heart] and He will come close to you" (James 4:8 AMP). Look who makes the first move.

You. God waits on *you*. He is the perfect gentleman. God doesn't force Himself on anyone.

In addition to hearing His voice and understanding myself better, I gained a multitude of benefits because of this exercise discipline. At that time in my life I was malnourished. I had an extremely poor diet that consisted of eating a bean-and-cheese burrito, nachos, and an extra-large sweet tea almost daily. But I ate hardly anything else the rest of the day, other than peanut butter crackers or maybe a Snickers bar. I would practically starve myself all day and then my big reward was eating my favorite meal: cheap, fast Mexican food.

But once I started exercising, I slept better, I started taking vitamins, I began drinking water instead of sweet tea with every meal, I gradually chose a salad over a burrito, my anxiety lifted, my mind was sharper, and as a bonus my body looked better than ever. Why would I even consider stopping something that provided a wealth of benefits? And that's exactly why it's still a part of my daily five.

Reduce It to the Ridiculous

I don't want you to get overwhelmed with all these tips, habits, and new disciplines when, if you're like me, your schedule is already jam-packed. How in the world are you supposed to do these five things before you head out the front door or to your home office to work?

I want to show you how to realistically get started on these five habits with five simple words: *reduce it to the ridiculous*. I learned this simple approach from John Assaraf, who shared it when he was asked how to teach people to become more disciplined.[11]

In other words, start small. Give yourself one command.

Could you wake up fifteen minutes earlier every day for ninety days?

Could you journal one thought every day for ninety days?

Could you drink one bottle of water every day for ninety days?

Could you read one page from a good book every day for ninety days?

Could you listen to one podcast while you're getting dressed every day for ninety days?

Reduce it to the ridiculous. You can do this. The question is, Will you?

When President John F. Kennedy asked Dr. Wernher von Braun what it would take to land a man on the moon and bring him safely back home, he replied, "The will to do it."[12] That seems like such a simple answer for such an enormous question. But your will to do things is the deciding factor.

The early bird does, in fact, catch the worm. When I joined the ranks of early risers and established those five simple habits in 2002, I never dreamed something so unspectacular would enable me to stand before presidents, launch books in several foreign languages, and speak in arenas of thousands of people simply sharing the secret of my success.

Today when people ask me, "How did your life change so drastically?" I simply say, "My morning routine."

I stopped rolling over and started rolling out at 5:00 a.m.

I stopped making excuses and started making time to pray.

I stopped scrolling through Facebook and started reading *books*.

I stopped listening to fear and started listening to motivational messages.

I stopped keeping up with the Kardashians and started keeping my commitment to work out.

I changed my morning routine, and it changed my whole life.

CHAPTER 9

Get Your Day Planned Before Bedtime

Life goals are reached by setting annual goals. Annual goals are reached by reaching daily goals. Daily goals are reached by doing things which may be uncomfortable at first but eventually become habits.
—JOHN MAXWELL

Zig Ziglar said that when he was a salesman, he had not been in the top five thousand in his sales company until he made a commitment to go to work on a regular schedule. At exactly 9:00 a.m., without fail, rain or shine, cold or hot, he was knocking on somebody's door. The interesting thing is that his wife would ask where he was going. And he would always say, "I've got an appointment." He never told her his appointment was with himself. The year he stuck with his commitments, he finished second out of seven thousand associates.[1]

Make appointments with yourself.

Maybe you're busier than ever and you desperately want these new habits in your life, but you don't know *when* you can realistically do all this.

I have the solution. It's called a calendar. Let me point out that scheduling things on your calendar is not about getting more things done—it's about getting the *right* things done.

I want to offer some ideas to help you feel a little more prepared and in control of your days instead of feeling out of control of your life. Take it or leave it—it's entirely up to your preferences for how organized you desire to be. The key to getting ahead is getting started.

1. Use One Planner or Calendar

Focus is the number one key ingredient to achieving your dreams and goals. To get focused, you need to get organized. I learned years ago to consistently record or document everything in *one* planner. Organizing expert Julie Morgenstern said, "You have one life; you need one planner."[2]

To keep things simple, record every important task, appointment, and reminder in one place. Don't use one planner for work, one for personal, one for your kids' agendas, one for your gym workouts, and one for meal planning. It would be exhausting trying to locate each one.

Whether it's digital or paper, use what works best for you. Some people need to touch and feel their work. They prefer to handwrite appointments and physically check off tasks completed. Others prefer to digitally document every reminder, keeping it neat and clean with no cancellations crossed out. They simply push Delete.

2. Write Everything Down

Don't rely on memory alone. Making a to-do list at the beginning of every day or every week can make you feel more focused and motivated to continue your work. If you make a list of all the things you must do, no matter how small, you will feel more accomplished when you check those items off your list and move on to the next task. First, it feels great to get all that stuff out of your head and onto paper. It's one of the best things you can do to relieve stress. And second, most of us instinctively love making checkmarks!

3. Practice the Sunday Night Strategy

Honestly, you can do this any hour and day of the week, but I always plan out my *entire week* on Sunday night. Even if I'm flying home from a meeting or after speaking on a Sunday morning somewhere, I never go to bed Sunday night without planning my entire week. It gives me an overview of exactly what I need to accomplish and how packed my schedule is. I can immediately see if I have time for any lunch appointments, doctor visits, playtime, errands, dinners with friends, and downtime.

Having your week thought out and organized sets you up to succeed. You'll no longer wake up wondering what the day may bring. You bring it. You arise Monday morning with vision and a plan, ready to succeed on purpose.

Personally, I make two different columns: Business Goals and Personal Goals (just for the week). I begin listing *every single thing* I can think of: pay bills, sort laundry, call dentist, get car washed, get birthday gift for nephew, return shirt, go to the bank, research vacations, lunch with my mom and dad, call my grandma, schedule a mani-pedi, and so on. The items don't have to be in chronological order of when I will take the actions; they just need to be thought out and written down.

After I have considered everything in my personal life to be done that week, then I do the same with my business goals. That list could include things such as prepare podcasts, tape podcasts, prepare for team meeting, conduct team meeting, review monthly letter, answer emails, sign thank-you cards, prepare four TV broadcasts, choose clothes for broadcasts, tape four broadcasts, prepare notes for weekend conference, and so forth.

You can start this process by making a list of everything you currently do or are currently responsible for, such as laundry, housecleaning, grocery shopping, paying bills, commuting, team meetings, phone calls, and the kids' dance lessons or soccer practice. Think of what tasks apply to your personal and professional life.

This practice has enabled me to be much more proactive rather than reactive in my business and personal life. There's hardly a day that I don't achieve what I set out to do because it's thoroughly planned.

4. Plan Each Day the Night Before

In addition to the Sunday-night strategy, you need an every-night strategy where you never go to bed without mapping out the next day. You simply go down your list of goals for the week and assign a day and time for each task.

A recent study found that spending five minutes writing your to-do list before bed leads to more peaceful sleep.[3] Out of 233 wealthy people interviewed by Tom Corley, 81 percent make a to-do list.[4] This habit helps you feel organized and in control of your life.

Once you review your list of to-dos, designate a specific day and time for each one to ensure it gets done. For example, if one of your personal goals for the week is to "Go online to research accounting classes" but you miss the vital step of assigning a day to do it, you'll keep skipping right over it. Weeks will go by, and you'll still be delaying your goal of getting an accounting degree. You must appoint a time to do it: Tuesday at noon. Always follow up your to-do item with a date and time![5]

Examples:

- Open savings account: Friday on lunch break.
- Make hair appointment: Tuesday at 10:00 a.m.
- Declutter kitchen: Sunday at 4:00 p.m.
- Do laundry: Saturday morning (approx. 8:00 a.m.)

5. Time Yourself

This is a two-step process.

1. Determine how long each task will take. After you see your daily schedule, you need to know approximately how much time is required to realistically complete the task. Many times we undercalculate the time needed and end up frustrated with how few of our goals were achieved that day. I used to make lists of forty-seven things to do and only finish nineteen by the end of the day. Nineteen! That's a lot to accomplish but I was still frustrated, mad at myself, and feeling unproductive. Why? My list was completely unrealistic. I thought I could write an article in two hours, but once I started timing myself, it was more like four hours (or more). I thought the phone call would last ten minutes but it was more like thirty minutes.

When I first began to apply this principle of timing how long each task really takes, it was pretty tedious. After a while I began to catch on and it enabled me to make my daily agendas more practical and attainable. This includes the time it takes to get ready each day, the time to commute, the time to prepare dinner, and so on. You may dread timing your tasks in the beginning, but trust me, it will lead to an extremely productive life.

2. Determine how much time you need to stay focused on a task. Deadlines are motivating, even twenty-minute ones. Because we live in such a distraction-filled society, it's a challenge to stay focused

on one task for even half an hour without checking our Facebook page, answering texts, or looking at photos on Instagram.

Give yourself sixty minutes to work on a certain task without any distractions—without even getting up. It's challenging, trust me. We're so accustomed to distractions. After one hour, check your phone or social media, go to the restroom, respond to the text, or grab a bite to eat. Then, do it again! Set the timer and get productive.

. . .

John Maxwell wrote *Today Matters*, a book that changed my life. The entire concept of the book is to place value on today. Success is not a destination; it's a journey. Maxwell describes how you go to college, finish all four years, and then the big graduation day comes. You walk across the stage, the president hands you the diploma, the photographer takes your picture, and the coliseum full of people applaud your accomplishment, confirming that you are successful!

Maxwell says that you did not become a success the day you got your diploma—you got *recognized* for success. The diploma is recognition for what you've done the previous four years. You were a success freshman year when you decided to not drop out like some of your friends. You were a success when you showed up for class when others slept in. You were a success when you turned in the projects, studied for exams, and put in the work. Maxwell wrote, "The secret of your success is determined by your daily agenda."[6]

What you want to be tomorrow, you've got to do today. And the success you will be recognized for takes place behind the scenes with nobody watching. Just waking up one hour earlier each day would give you an extra fifteen days each year.[7] What could you accomplish with an extra two weeks added to your life?

Behind-the-Scenes Habits
That Drive Crazy Success

HABIT #3

Wake up earlier, plan out your days, and keep your commitments to yourself. It's the alone advantage that leads to mastering self-discipline.

Very early in the morning, while it was still dark, Jesus got up, left the house and went off to a solitary place, where he prayed.
—MARK 1:35 NIV

PART 4

Grow Up!

CHAPTER 10

You Can't Have the Marshmallow

It doesn't matter what profession a person pursues,
thinking precedes achievement. . . . The greater
your thinking, the greater your potential.
—JOHN MAXWELL

I received this heart-gripping letter from a precious woman, Barbara, who was hiding from her abuser:

> Years ago, I was in a shelter for battered women. I was a single mom trying to flee my abuser. I was there with my toddler, and we had nothing but the clothes on our backs. I lost sight of all hope. In the shelter, I was assigned a mattress to sleep on. One night, I felt a bump under the mattress, and as I looked underneath, I found one of Terri's books.

Fast-forward seven years after Barbara read the book (about dreaming and making a vision board) to when she sent me this letter:

> My entire life changed. I've been able to accomplish nearly everything on my vision board. The trials I went through led me to Jesus. I now work in a church, have a small business, received my master's degree, I'm remarried to a man who respects me, and my son is now ten years old, doing well, and we are free from fear.

I am not taking credit for the drastic turnaround in Barbara's life, and I don't know how one of my books ended up under a mattress at a homeless shelter (though I'm so grateful it did). But this story proves the power of the written word to transform our lives.

Dr. Seuss may have said it best in his simple rhyme: "The more that you read, the more things you will know. The more that you learn, the more places you'll go."[1]

Did you know that someone else has already provided a blueprint for you to follow for whatever you're going through? A book is literally the advice, the experience, the wisdom of someone, just as if they were sitting down with you and sharing everything they know in person. Basically, through books you get to choose the mentors who will have the greatest impact on who you become.

If you want to live a healthier life, you can learn directly from health and wellness expert Dr. Don Colbert. Whether you want to overcome chronic pain, lose weight, or slow down the aging process, there's no appointment necessary. With more than forty books written from forty years of medical practice, through Dr. Colbert you have access to valuable wisdom to help you live long and strong.

If you would like to have better relationships with your spouse or children, Gary Smalley has poured decades of research and practical insights into his books that have helped millions of couples and parents. Chances are that the answers you need are found on the pages of one of his classic books.

If you are determined to get your finances in order, get out of debt, and build wealth, there is a book for that. Dave Ramsey provides a step-by-step formula in his bestselling book *The Total Money Makeover*. He shares his personal story from filing for bankruptcy to now experiencing financial peace and prosperity. His personal struggle with money gives you the shortcut to getting out of financial ruin and learning to save, invest, and budget wisely. What took him twenty years to learn you can acquire in one month by reading.

If you desire to be a better leader, start a company, or pastor a church, John Maxwell has more than seventy books of, in my opinion, the greatest wisdom ever given on leadership and personal growth. You don't have to make all the mistakes trying to figure it out on your own. You can learn to build teams, set goals, cast vision, and grow your company by reading a few pages a day.

You can get your home organized with Julie Morgenstern, learn how to invest with Warren Buffett, improve your thinking with Napoleon Hill, learn to manage with Peter Drucker, become a creative home entertainer with Martha Stewart, remove a few strokes on the golf course with Jack Nicklaus, learn about fashion with Anna Wintour, and even remodel your house with Chip and Joanna Gaines!

Whether it's pregnancy, gardening, writing, retirement planning, or spiritual growth, you have access to the knowledge you need to excel. Whichever area you want to improve, experts in their field have laboriously poured their life study into the pages of books available to you. Find your mentors inside the pages of their books.

ı ı ı

In an interview on the mindset of a winner, the late Kobe Bryant said, "Everything, everything, everything was done to try to become a better basketball player."[2] He went on to explain how he achieved that goal: "When you have that point of view, the world becomes your library to help you become better at your craft."[3] He then said, "I went to G.O.A.T. mountain."[4]

He got the advice he needed from the Greatest Of All Time— the GOATs—of basketball. You can do the same thing within the pages of books. For example, if you desire to be a comedian, can you imagine getting to sit down with Steve Martin and learning everything you can about stand-up comedy? You can. Steve tells it all in his autobiography, *Born Standing Up: A Comic's Life.*

What about a dream to play tennis professionally? Why not learn more from Wimbledon winner and tennis Hall of Famer Andre Agassi by reading his autobiography *Open*? You can learn about running a business from the founder of the world's largest retailer, Sam Walton, in his book *Sam Walton: Made in America*. Why not study how to tap into your full potential by reading Tony Robbins's classic, *Awaken the Giant Within*? Or discover how the favor of God can be produced in your life from books by my favorite preacher, Jerry Savelle? The opportunities to learn from the best are endless, and they are at your fingertips inside the pages of their memoirs and study guides to success.

Here's my point: you can't grow anymore on what you've learned up to now. It brought you this far. You'll have to keep feeding on fresh information if you want to go to a new level. I heard someone say, "If you don't adopt the mindset that you can never learn enough, sooner or later whatever you have learned won't be enough."

> If you don't adopt the mindset that you can never learn enough, sooner or later whatever you have learned won't be enough.

It was December 1991 in Lubbock, Texas, when I placed my graduation cap on top of my big, Texas-size hair and wore my black gown adorned with red tassels, symbolizing my achievement of graduating *cum laude* from Texas Tech University. It was the day I had been counting down to witness for fifty-two months (I was on the four-and-a-half-year plan). It was college graduation day.

"Terri Lynn Savelle, Bachelor of Arts." That was my cue to walk across the stage in a coliseum of seven thousand people and receive my award for four years of studying the French language (my major) and learning how to communicate effectively (my minor). This was my moment of payoff! I'd put in the hours, crammed for exams, and I now had the proof of my discipline to hang proudly on the wall.

A few hours later, the entire Savelle family joined up at El Chico in west Texas for our traditional Tex-Mex feast to celebrate my accomplishment. As we ate the bottomless bowl of chips and salsa and ordered another round of bean-and-cheese nachos, I made a bold yet idiotic declaration to my family: "I will never study again!" I mean, why would I? I had the degree. I'd graduated with honors. I knew all I needed to know. *It's good enough to last me forever*, I thought with ridiculous logic.

.   .   .

The announcement of my ignorance to the family that day was probably the dumbest thing I have ever said. But what's worse is that it became the dumbest commitment I ever kept. I literally "backed up" the dumb promise of never studying for eleven years of my life! For more than a decade, I didn't pick up another book. I never listened to a motivational teaching (other than attending church on Sundays). I never invested in a conference. I never gleaned from a mentor, listened to an audiobook, or downloaded a podcast. Nothing. I pretty much *never studied again*! And my life proved it.

As I mentioned in the introduction of this book, I lived paycheck to paycheck. I paid my car note every month. I paid my credit cards faithfully. I had nothing in my savings account. I spent everything I earned. I woke up at the last minute to rush to the office and was the first to leave at 5:00 p.m. so I could hurry home and watch other people live their dreams—aka watch TV.

In 2002, when I finally got desperate for change, I set my alarm a little bit earlier, went for my morning walk, came back to the quiet, dark house, journaled my time in prayer, and sat down in my den with a book. That was so foreign to me. I picked up one book and started with one page, one day at a time. I set the alarm on my phone for twenty minutes and forced myself to start a new success habit.

Gradually something surprising began to happen. The more I read, the more I wanted to learn. Little by little, I was learning everything from how to manage my time to how to reduce my debt, how to lead an organization, how to get my body in shape, how to build my confidence, and how to set goals for my future.

I had enlightening things to share with my coworkers when I got to the office. I had learned so much before I even pulled into the parking lot. People around me started asking, "How do you know this stuff?" By a simple dose of twenty minutes every morning while the rest of the world still tossed and turned.

The more I learned, the more I began to earn. As a result, during the next eleven years of my life, my income quadrupled, my cars were paid off, my credit card debt was paid in full, my savings account was healthy, and my investment portfolio was starting to grow. I went from proudly declaring I would never read again to inspiring millions to build a personal library.

Bottom line: as I began to grow, everything around me grew. My life has seen enormous increase and success due to getting up before dawn and reading the pages of good books. People are truly rewarded in public for what they practice in private. Napoleon Hill said, "The person who stops studying merely because they have finished school is forever hopelessly doomed to mediocrity, no matter what their calling."[5]

.   .   .

In his bestselling book *See You at the Top*, Zig Ziglar asked,

Do you plan to eat tomorrow? If you do, does that mean what you ate today was no good? Absolutely not. It simply means what you ate today is for today. The average person in America not only eats every day but he eats his meals on schedule. I've observed if a person gets busy and misses a meal, he tells anyone who will listen, "You know what? I was so busy yesterday I didn't have time to eat lunch." Then he repeats it to make certain his listener got the message. . . . Suppose the same individual was asked about his mental appetites? "When is the last time you deliberately, on a pre-determined schedule, fed your own mind?" What do you think his answer would be? . . . From the neck down, very few people are worth more than a few hundred dollars a week. From the neck up, there is no limit to what an individual is worth.[6]

Everything in your life stops growing when your mind stops growing. I want to give you, in the sweetest way possible, the message I had to come to grips with: *grow up!*

If you will simply read twenty minutes each day, you will have read approximately eighteen books in a year's time.[7]

Ralph Waldo Emerson mentored Henry David Thoreau, and every time they would meet Emerson asked what Thoreau had learned since they last met.[8] Ask yourself: *What did I do last year to grow?*

How many books did you read? How many hours of TV do you think you watched each day? If you were to cut out one hour, as Jack Canfield did, do you think it would benefit you? (I'm pretty sure it would, dramatically!)

Michael Jordan's trainer, Tim Grover, said, "The body has limitations, the mind does not."[9]

Warning: when you begin the habit of getting up early and setting aside time to read, your mind will tell you to keep sleeping: *You have so far to go—what's the point in getting up before the sun? How is twenty minutes going to change your life? Can I just keep sleeping and read later today?* I had those same conversations going on in my head. Let me tell you about eating marshmallows.

. . .

Years ago, behavioral scientists took children into a classroom and offered them one marshmallow to eat right on the spot. However, they said, "If you wait to eat the marshmallow until we tell you to, then you can have two marshmallows."

When the children's responses were later categorized, they fell into three groups.

The first group, which made up one-third of the kids, shoved the marshmallows in their mouths instantly. They could not wait. They had to have their marshmallows right then. Instant gratification was their natural tendency.

The second group, which made up another one-third of the kids, decided to wait. They naturally had the behavior of delaying gratification with ease.

The third group, which made up the final one-third of the kids, were very interesting. They desperately wanted the first marshmallow, but they equally had a strong desire to get two marshmallows. The struggle was real. They didn't have the natural tendency to just patiently wait, so they turned their chairs around so they couldn't see the temptation. They made funny faces and tried to distract themselves from thinking about the marshmallows. They literally forced themselves to delay their desire and they ended up being rewarded with two.

- Group one: instant gratification
- Group two: naturally delayed gratification
- Group three: naturally programmed to be group one but fought with themselves until they became group two

Here's what the researchers discovered when they followed up with these children years later. Those in groups two and three were far more successful than group one. The point being that it doesn't matter if you're naturally equipped to delay your rewards like group two; what matters is that you can train yourself to become group two.[10]

It all boils down to delaying gratification. I call it the "Pay now, play later" principle. Get up early, do the hard things, pay the price so you can play later.

CHAPTER 11

What Successful People Do in Traffic

If you can train yourself to do what you should do,
when you should do it, whether you feel like it or
not, your success is virtually guaranteed.
—ANONYMOUS

jumped in my beautiful black Mercedes one Saturday morning to run a few quick errands. By the time I got home and the rest of the family woke up, I had paid off my car! *What happened?* you ask. *Did you win the scratch-off at the convenience store?* No, I got something better. During that short forty-five-minute trek to the bank and the car wash, I got the wisdom I needed to be debt-free.

Let me explain. I was listening to financial expert Dave Ramsey as I drove across town that morning. He made a simple statement stressing the importance of living without debt and not wasting money on interest charges every month. Then he said that if you have the money in your savings account to pay off your car, but you're leaving that money in there to feel secure, then drain the savings. He shouted, "You're wasting money paying your car note every month along with that interest payment! Pay off the car now! Today! Then build your savings account back up."[1]

I was so proud of myself for finally having a savings account that I didn't want to drain it. But Dave's wisdom made such sense. I owed around $14,000 on my car and I had approximately $16,000 saved. I went online, transferred the money, and paid off my car that very day. And then I went to work on building my savings back up, starting with the money I used to spend on the car payment. The car drove a little smoother after that day.

What am I saying? The most successful people in the world go to "automobile university." They use their drive time to listen and learn. They grow as they go—everywhere. It could be five minutes to drop off their dry cleaning or thirty minutes to the office. It could be waiting in line to pick up their kids at school or waiting for a train to pass—they utilize every opportunity to grow, learn, and improve their mindset for success. Tom Corley wrote in his book *Rich Habits* that 63 percent of wealthy people listen to audio books during their commutes to work.[2]

This is by far the easiest habit to adopt into your current routine to drastically change your thinking and retrain your mind. It requires very little effort on your part, but the results are some of the most rewarding.

As I shared how this habit began years ago while cleaning my house, I purposefully got my hands on some encouraging audio messages that I could listen to consistently. Your thinking must change for your life to change. Everything gets its start in the mind. In theory that's great, but how do you renew your mind? Again, the number one method God has given us to start this practice is found in Romans 10:17: "Faith comes by hearing, and hearing by the word of God" (NKJV).

As I mentioned in part 2, I was not disciplined so I needed all the help I could get and the reminders I could find to keep me on track. My hot pink Post-it Note with the words *push Play* stuck on my bathroom mirror was my first step in developing this life-changing habit.

This morning ritual inspired me to seize every opportunity I could find to hear more. I was getting smarter every time I drove my little girl to school, loaded the dishwasher, folded the laundry, made the beds, deposited my paycheck at the bank, and went to and from work while everybody else was singing their favorite songs.

My mind has truly been renewed and my life has been improved in phenomenal ways due to this elementary habit that requires a minimal amount of discipline. You don't have to allocate time on your schedule. You don't have to stop what you're doing. You don't even have to force yourself to exert more energy than you're currently expending. You just use your pointer and middle finger and press the little arrow-shaped button until you hear something audible. Ha! It's mind-boggling what those two fingers can produce in your life.

You've probably heard the phrase that whatever isn't feeding you is depleting you. You can't fill your mind with negative input and expect to live a positive life. Every time you hear God's Word, your faith grows. Faith is what you desperately need to live your dreams. Faith is the "medicine" required to overcome your fears. If your fears are stopping you from your dreams, *push Play.*

Get Motivated In Thirty Seconds

I'll never forget one morning in 2004 when I woke up discouraged. For whatever reason, my mind was focused more on the bad memories of my past than on my dreams for the future. I went through my morning routine, drove to work, and walked into my office still not fully encouraged. As I was sitting at my desk going through the motions, a coworker walked in and asked if I wanted to view the new opening segment for the TV broadcast we were launching. Since I led the media department, it was part of my job to approve or disapprove programming changes.

I walked into the editing room, he pushed Play, and this is what I heard shouting across the screen and through the speakers:

"Don't you ever say again that you can't take any more! You can take anything the enemy dishes out! You're a child of the Most High God! You're not a victim. You're a victor! The blood of Jesus flows through your veins. You're a champion. Hallelujah!"[3]

In less than thirty seconds my mindset changed. Listening to that powerful, high-energy, motivational clip, I left the editing room with a completely different outlook on my life. I was able to get control over my mood, my emotions, and my negative thinking and shift my thoughts in a positive direction—in less than one minute! That's the power of listening and retraining your mind by hearing God's truths.

Whatever you're feeling most compelled to study right now, that's where you need to focus your time, money, resources, and attention. Where do you need to spend the most time gaining knowledge? Become a serious student in that area.

Set yourself up for success by researching the resources you need. Be ready tomorrow morning when you head off for your normal commute. Whether it's downloading an audiobook or a podcast or ordering resources online, get it ready to go.

One study reported that the average person commutes thirty minutes to and from work each day. Over a five-year period, that's 1,250 hours behind the wheel of your car (and additional time to learn).[4] Can you believe that?

ABC News published an article titled "Here's How Much Time Americans Waste in Traffic" by Erin Dooley. It's all in how you view time: it's wasting time to moan about the traffic; instead you can seize that time to learn everything you can. The article shared startling statistics of how many hours Americans spend stuck in traffic jams each year, with the average being forty-two hours. That's not including the commute time—that's just hours spent at a standstill on the road.[5]

The most congested city in the United States is currently Chicago, showing their annual average is 155 hours of delay with nothing to do—but grow! I see that as optimal time to get ahead, accelerate your knowledge, and grow by leaps and bounds. Think of how much those in Boston (the second-most congested city) get to learn in those precious 134 hours on the road. Or New Yorkers in 117 hours and Philadelphia residents in 114 hours each year.[6]

The Bible says, "Study to shew thyself approved" (2 Timothy 2:15 KJV). You can no longer justify your excuse for not learning by saying you don't have time. Just turn your car into a classroom. The late UCLA basketball coach John Wooden said, "If I am through learning, I am through."[7] Success is the result of just a few small disciplines practiced daily. This is one that will speed up your results.

There's an inspiring story in the Bible about Joseph, who had an incredible dream and a remarkable life. He saved an entire nation. He set up a legacy for his family. The short version is this: As a young man around seventeen, Joseph had a dream, and he communicated it to his brothers. They got extremely jealous, threw him into a pit, and then sold him into slavery.

Thirteen long years went by without seeing his brothers or his brothers seeing him. Until one day when Joseph's family experienced a severe famine. They didn't have any food, and they heard there was plenty in Egypt, so they decided to humble themselves and go ask for food.

My friend Joel Sims pointed out his interpretation of this scripture, and I want to share it with you. After thirteen years "although Joseph recognized his brothers, they did not recognize him" (Genesis 42:8). Think about that. More than a decade went by, and Joseph looked at his brothers and instantly recognized one by one who they were. How can that be? Joel says it's because they were exactly the same. The brothers looked right into Joseph's eyes, and none of them identified him as their own blood. Why? Because he had changed. He grew. He matured. Joseph was not the same kid they threw in the pit that day. But nothing about the brothers had changed.

In life, you can be like Joseph, or you can be like his brothers. The only way to do what God has called you to do is if you *grow up*. Never cease your quest for knowledge. Over the next twelve months, become unrecognizable to everyone around you.

CHAPTER 12

Get Your Library Started

I ought to be able to look in your surroundings and know
your dream. Are the books you're reading taking you to
your dream? Is what you're doing in private taking you
to where you want to be? Is where you're spending your
money taking you closer to your dream? Show me your
checking account and I'll show you your priorities.
—ATTRIBUTED TO BISHOP T. D. JAKES

ast week a letter was on my desk, written by a man named Den
Slattery who shared this amazing true story:

One cold winter morning a man was walking down a street
in Cleveland, Ohio. The wind was blowing, and it was snowing
lightly. As he walked, he came to a pawn shop and saw something
in the window that caught his attention. As he looked at the object,
he said to himself, "There is the answer to all my problems."

As he thought about his life, he realized that he had lost everything because of his drinking. His job, his house, his wife, and his
only daughter. The only thing he had left was his car, which he was
sleeping in. Other than that, he was just another drunken bum on
the street. But that object in the window could change everything.

As he stared at it, he could see himself with a bottle in one hand and that gun in his other hand. He could put it to his head and pull the trigger and all his problems would be gone. No one would care. Life would go on without missing a beat.

Just at that moment, the wind picked up and he felt a shiver. He wanted to get out of this cold, but the pawn shop was closed. So, he walked down the street and found a library that was open. He went in and sat at a table.

As he warmed up, he decided to get something to read. His mom had instilled in him a love for books. As he was looking for a book, he found one on success and sat down to read it. The book that really caught his attention was written by W. Clement Stone. It was called *Success Through a Positive Mental Attitude.*

He read the whole book and then read it again, and again, and again. He saw that book as a gift from God.

The man in this true story, Og Mandino, went from wanting to kill himself to working for W. Clement Stone and becoming one of the pioneers in personal development, selling more than fifty million books worldwide.

It's All About Growth

Jim Rohn said that any time someone told him that they wanted to be a success, he would say something like, "Great. Take me to your house and show me your library." Why? According to Rohn, "The reason is because what a man reads pours massive ingredients into his mental factory and the fabric of his life is built from those ingredients."[1] You must have an endless thirst for knowledge if you want to rise above mediocrity.

The Bible says, "From everyone who has been given much, much will be demanded" (Luke 12:48). You could rephrase this by saying,

"Much is *required* in order for much to be *given*." In other words, to have more you simply must become more.

When I teach this concept at conferences, I typically hold up a giant (fake) one-hundred-dollar bill and quote Jim Rohn, who is known for making the statement, "Your money will only grow to the extent that you grow. If you don't like the size of your money—increase the size of you!"

You could apply that phrase to anything in life.

Your *career* will only grow to the extent that you grow.

Your *ministry* will only grow to the extent that you grow.

Your *opportunities* will only grow to the extent that you grow.

Your *relationships* will only grow to the extent that you grow.

Your *vacations* will only grow to the extent that you grow.

When John Maxwell was asked, "What's the number one predictor that you will be successful?" without hesitating, he responded, "Be intentional about your personal growth."[2]

A lot of people have good intentions but they're not intentional about growing. What could you accomplish if you were strategic about growing yourself? I'm asking you to dedicate yourself to a new level of learning and studying. What are you doing intentionally to be certain your life is different ninety days from now? Which books are you going to read? Which messages are you going to listen to? Which courses are you enrolling in?

In his book *The Millionaire Next Door*, Thomas Stanley shares the startling statistic that 80–85 percent of millionaires in the United States are self-made.[3] And one reason why a person becomes a millionaire is often because they are open to learning and personal growth. Bottom line: if you want a remarkable life, you've got to pay a remarkable price.

You must invest in your personal growth.

The 3 Percent Rule

I just learned about the 3 percent rule from Brian Tracy. I had the honor of going to his house, having dinner with him, and absorbing what he wanted to share.

Tracy said, "To guarantee your lifelong success, make a decision today to invest 3 percent of your income back into yourself. This seems to be the magic number of lifelong learning. The payoff is extraordinary!"

For example, if your annual income is $50,000, then 3 percent is $1,500 that you need to invest back into yourself to upgrade your knowledge. Tracy also tells this story:

> I was giving a seminar in Detroit a couple years ago when a young man, about thirty years old, came up to me at the break. He told me that he had . . . heard my "3 Percent Rule" about ten years ago. At that time, he had dropped out of college, was living at home, driving an old car, and earning about $20,000 a year as a salesman.
>
> He decided after the seminar that he was going to apply the 3 Percent Rule to himself. . . . He calculated 3 percent of his income of $20,000 would be $600. He began to buy sales books and read them every day. He invested in two audio-learning programs. He invested the entire $600 in himself. . . .
>
> That year, his income went from $20,000 to $30,000, an increase of 50 percent. . . .
>
> So the following year, he invested 3 percent of $30,000, a total of $900, back into himself. That year, his income jumped from $30,000 to $50,000. He began to think, "If my income goes up at 50 percent per year by investing 3 percent back into myself, what would happen if I invested 5 percent?"
>
> The next year, he invested 5 percent of his income, $2,500, into his learning program. He took more seminars, traveled

cross-country to a conference, bought more audio- and video-learning programs, and even hired a part-time coach. And that year, his income *doubled* to $100,000.

After that, like playing Texas Hold'em, he decided to go "all in" and raise his investment into himself to 10 percent per year. He told me that he has been doing this ever since.

I asked him, "How has investing 10 percent of your income back into yourself affected your income?"

He smiled and said, "I passed a million dollars in personal income last year."[4]

I will never forget the first time I put some of my own money on the line to obtain new audio teachings and books. After I had practically worn out my parents' audios that I sorta stole from their house, it was time for some new messages. Because I was vividly seeing for myself the positive impact that investing in my growth was having on my life, I wanted more. I went online to a minister's website and went on a shopping spree for wisdom.

It was like a smorgasbord of motivation: "How to Build Your Confidence," "How to Overcome Fear and Doubt," "The Keys to a Successful Mindset," "Break Free from Your Past," and "The Power of Determination." All I could think was "add to cart." However, I was shocked when the total came to sixty dollars! Remember, this was back in 2002. *Sixty dollars? I'm not going to spend sixty bucks on faith-building resources! This is ridiculous!*

But I instantly thought, *I would easily spend this amount on new clothes. This is helping me get a new mindset! My future is worth sixty dollars!* and I pushed Payment.

When that little brown box arrived at the front door, I thought I had struck a gold mine. I could hardly wait to run upstairs to my giant boom box, put in the CD, and start learning! Today I can honestly say that the most valuable items in my house are not my luxury handbags, designer shoes, or the stunning diamond ring Rodney bought me for our twenty-fifth wedding anniversary (sorry, Rod). My most prized possessions are the items on my shelf in my personal library! Those audios, books, and resources stacked in my home office are what transformed my life from the inside out.

When I sit at a table to discuss marketing ideas, financial investing, spiritual guidance, the benefits of fasting, leading teams in personal growth, or even twenty-one ways to use a resistance band, I have something valuable to say! Like those coworkers at the office used to do, I've had friends ask, "How do you know all this stuff?" By a simple act of *push Play* each morning while I add more eye shadow and while I drive through Rockwall, Texas, on my way to work.

You can't put a price on transformation. We tend to invest in the latest appliances, the daily latte, the mani-pedi, and the dinner outings with friends, but far too often we neglect the greatest use of our finances, which is investing in ourselves. Unlike other investments out there, investing in yourself is never a risk. It always pays off.

What is a successful mindset programmed for greatness worth to you? When you invest in yourself, a whole new world of opportunities will open for you. Go online to the websites of those you admire, those you connect with and relate to. Get everything they have to offer. Subscribe to their podcasts. Download their audios. Read their books. Go to their conferences. Invest in your promising new future. It's the best money you will ever spend.

The largest room in the world is the room for improvement. Make you and your growth a priority every day. How? Start building your very own personal library.

Behind-the-Scenes Habits That Drive Crazy Success

HABIT #4

Grow up by setting a goal to invest in your personal growth. Read something positive twenty minutes a day, and turn your car into a classroom by listening to audiobooks during your commute. It's the alone advantage that leads to personal growth.

Wise men and women are always learning, always listening for fresh insights.
—PROVERBS 18:15 MSG

PART 5

Look Up!

CHAPTER 13

Can You Imagine?

Imagination should be used, not to escape reality, but to create it.
—COLIN WILSON

Have you heard swimming coach Bob Bowman share about how Michael Phelps became one of the most decorated and famous athletes in history? Yes, he had incredible routines and rituals that caused him to rise above the competition, but he also used his imagination and visualized his races daily. After practice Phelps would do what Bowman called "watching the videotape" both before bed and first thing in the morning.

Charles Duhigg explains: "The videotape wasn't real. Rather, it was a mental visualization of the perfect race. Each night before falling asleep and each morning after waking up, Phelps would imagine himself jumping off the blocks and, in slow motion, swimming flawlessly."

Then when Phelps went to practice, his coach would shout, "Put in the videotape!" when he wanted Phelps to give it everything he had.[1]

Michael Phelps knew that without a mental picture of where he was headed, he'd stay confined within his limitations—even though he had the potential to go further. And that's exactly where I was for eleven years until I learned this private habit.

You will never leave where you are until you see where you would rather be in your imagination. Everything gets its start in the imagination.

• • •

God told Abraham to *look up* from where he currently lived to a land that He would show him. He was instructing Abraham to use his God-given imagination. Today God is telling you to look up from where you are to the remarkable future He has planned for you.

When was the last time you sat quietly in a room and looked up? In other words, when was the last time you gave your heart permission to dream? If you're like I was, I hadn't used my imagination since I was a child, when I would imagine I was on a deserted island like movie star Ginger on *Gilligan's Island*, wearing sequined dresses and lots of makeup out in the middle of nowhere. I would also imagine that I was Farrah Fawcett from the TV show *Charlie's Angels* or that I was on the sidelines of NFL football games performing as a Dallas Cowboys cheerleader. But as I grew up I stopped using that God-given gift of imagination.

> Visualize the person you desire to become. Set aside time each day to be alone and undisturbed. . . . See yourself in this new environment, capable and self-confident.
> —MARY KAY ASH

Michael Todd said, "Don't belittle your imagination! It's God-given. It's divine. Those daydreams could be God trying to show you a glimpse of the future that is possible for you if you would only believe Him enough to move toward it."[2]

To stress the importance of having a dream, let's see what happens when you don't. God's Word says, "Where there is no vision, the people perish" (Proverbs 29:18 KJV). Steve Harvey said, "Most often, perishing is a slow, painful process, and if you aren't paying attention, it will trick you into thinking that this is the way things are supposed to be. . . . When you sit by and just let your life perish without a vision, it is the most painful kind of death."[3]

Never stop dreaming. Never stop using your imagination. Never get comfortable where you are. When you stop dreaming, you start dying. Look at what the cost of not having a vision can produce in your life.

In John Maxwell's book *Be All You Can Be*, he shares these startling truths:

> When Alexander the Great had a vision, he conquered countries; when he lost it, he couldn't conquer a liquor bottle. When David had a vision, he conquered Goliath; and when he lost his vision, he couldn't conquer his own lust. When Samson had a vision, he won many battles; when he lost his vision, he couldn't win a battle with Delilah. When Solomon had a vision, he was the wisest man in the world; when he lost the dream God had given him, he couldn't control his own evil passion for foreign women. When Saul had a vision, he could conquer kings; when he lost his vision, he couldn't conquer his own jealousy. When Noah had a vision, he could build an ark and help keep the human race on track; when he lost his vision, he got drunk. When Elijah had a vision, he could pray down fire from heaven and chop off the heads of false prophets; when he lost the dream, he ran from Jezebel. It's the dream that keeps us young; it's the vision that keeps us going.[4]

Although I began developing these life-changing habits in private, it wasn't until 2006 that I truly looked up and gave my heart permission to dream as big as I could. In the privacy of my little bedroom with nobody around but God and me, and with no knowledge of just how powerful the God-given imagination is, I sat down quietly with a journal and a pen and began to visualize my ideal life.

I began thinking beyond my present reality of getting the laundry done or the living room organized—I was really designing my destiny. I was embarrassed to admit what I thought I saw in my future because I felt so unqualified and ridiculous thinking that I had the right to dream this big.

Brian Tracy calls this practice "back from the future" thinking. He recommends that you project your life five years into the future and imagine that it is perfect in every way. What does it look like? What is the year? How old are you? If you're married, how long have you been married? If you have children, add five years to their current age. What is your ideal life in every respect five years from today?[5]

On August 16, 2006, I sat there in silence and let my imagination run wild as if it were August 2011, five years into my future. I imagined what I would have accomplished if I truly believed anything was possible and listed them: (1) minister on TV, (2) write a book, (3) host a women's conference, (4) start an outreach to young women rescued from human trafficking, and (5) start a mission in France. Each of these crazy dreams was far outside the realm of possibility, but for some reason, once I took the time to get them out of my head (full of doubt) and onto paper (full of possibilities), my potential began to rise.

It was almost as if I were sitting behind the wheel of a car with no destination in mind until that very moment, on August 16, 2006, when I "programmed my GPS" (allowed my subconscious mind to pinpoint my route to get to my dream destination). Almost instantly my life began to move in the direction of the words in that spiral notebook.

Within five years' time every single impossible dream in that notebook was a reality in my life. By August 16, 2011 (five years later), I was cohosting a weekly television broadcast with my dad. I had already written two books and witnessed seeing them on the shelves in my local bookstore. In 2010 I launched a women's conference called ICING, which has grown to thousands of women. I started reaching out to girls' homes, safe houses, and shelters for young women, giving them my books and resources to help them get a vision for their lives. In 2008 I began ministering in the nation of France and found a French publisher who translates all my books into French. Here's the kicker: not one single dream took even the full five years to accomplish.

. . .

John Maxwell says, "The value of a vision is that it encourages you to give up at any moment all that you are in order to receive all that you can become. In other words, once you've had a glimpse of what God can make of you, you'll never be satisfied with what you now are."[6] I'm convinced the next five years could be the most amazing, most phenomenal, and most rewarding years of your life—or they could be just another five years. It's entirely up to you.

"I have chosen you and have not rejected you" (Isaiah 41:9). "Before I shaped you in the womb, I knew all about you. Before you saw the light of day, I had holy plans for you" (Jeremiah 1:5 MSG). God has plans for your life. Isn't it time you discover them and live them out?

1. Imagine Five Years from Now

Robert Collier is quoted as saying, "Visualize this thing that you want. See it, feel it, believe in it. Make your mental blueprint and begin to build." Sit quietly and imagine your ideal life five years into the future. You must see the end from the beginning. That's the way God works. He said, "I make known the end from the beginning" (Isaiah 46:10).

It's five years from today and you can have anything you want. What can you imagine?

- Are you married?
- Do you have a baby?
- Are your kids in college?

- Are you working? Where?
- What do you look like? Do you have an image of what you want to look like physically? See yourself from head to toe. Are you fit, healthy, and feeling alive?
- What are you driving? What color is it? Can you see yourself in it?
- What is your financial condition like? Are you saving money consistently? How much do you have saved by now? What is that exact number? Are you satisfied with that?
- Where do you live? Is it the same house you live in now? Have you moved? Are you living in a different city or state or country? Where is it? Is it on the lake? Is it on a large piece of property? Or a condo in the city? Is it near the beach or the mountains?
- Where have you been? Have you traveled? Are you enjoying life and all there is to see? Have you been to Paris, Tokyo, or Rome? What are those places you've read about and dreamed of seeing?
- What have you accomplished? Did you finish that article and submit it to the local newspaper? Did you finish that accounting class at the local college? Did you start that catering business? Did you go to the fashion institute? Did you learn how to create your own website? Can you speak French or Spanish fluently now? Did you start that side job that's generating an extra $10,000 annually?
- Are you ministering? Are you teaching a class? Did you write your first book? Did you go on your first mission trip? Is your debt paid off?
- What does your ideal life look like five years from now?

What are some of those dreams you had when you were a child? What about when you first became an adult? Are you living the life you imagined? If not, why? What is stopping you? Why can't you go back and get that college degree? Five years from now, you could have it. Why can't you take those flying lessons? Sign up for an evening or weekend class. Five years from now, you could be flying planes, earning a larger salary, making new friendships, exposing yourself to the world. Have you always wanted to get your Realtor's license and sell houses? Do it now. Five years from now you could be living a completely different lifestyle. What's stopping you?

No matter how big or how small the dream may seem, it's still a dream. It's a goal and it's a vision. And it's needed to keep you alive and living your life to the fullest! Close your eyes and visualize where you see yourself five years from today.

2. Write It Down

"Write the vision; make it plain" (Habakkuk 2:2 ᴇsᴠ). This isn't difficult; however, what's easy to do is also easy *not* to do. It's as simple as picking up the closest pen, grabbing a notebook, and starting to write.

Be specific about what you see. Don't just write, "I want to make a lot of money over the next five years." Your mind doesn't know how to define "a lot," so it has nothing to aim toward. Vague goals produce vague results. Be very specific about how you define "a lot." It could be, "I have $50,000 saved in the next five years." That means you need to start saving $10,000 each year or $834 each month or $192 each week. That's a clear vision.

Clarity is one of the single most important keys to success. James Clear said, "Many people think they lack motivation, when what they really lack is clarity."[7] "Clarity is power. The more clear you are about what you want, the more likely you are to achieve it," Billy Cox agrees.[8]

When I had dinner with Brian Tracy last spring in San Diego, he looked at me over his bowl of clam chowder and said emphatically, "As soon as you have a dream, write it down, write it down, write it down." Got it!

3. Make a Vision Board or Vision Book

"Are you surprised at what God has done in your life and ministry?" I get this question a lot, especially from those who knew me before or know my story of how painfully insecure I was before I began these habits of solitude.

My answer is the same every time: "I am truly overwhelmed with gratitude. I think I say, 'Thank You, Jesus' at least seventy-five times a day because I am so grateful for what God has done and I never take it for granted. But I'm not surprised."

> You've got to create dream boards. If you can see it in your mind, you can hold it in your hand.
> —ATTRIBUTED TO STEVE HARVEY

I'm not saying that to sound arrogant. The reason I'm not surprised is because everything that's happening in my life and through our ministry right now are things that I dreamed about in my journals. I've simply applied God's principles for success. So why should I be surprised?

I only know how to teach something through my own experience, so I want to build your faith with some of my own stories. God can make things happen for you that you could never make happen on your own when you start getting clear on your dreams and putting them in front of you.

For example, one day I wrote down five foreign languages into which I wanted my books translated. One of them was German. I don't know anybody in Germany. I don't speak German. At the time I'd never even been to Germany. But German was one of the languages I had on my heart. So, I put a map of Germany on my vision board.

Let's see what God's Word says. "You may ask me for anything in my name, and I will do it" (John 14:14). It is no coincidence that seven months after I wrote down that vision, we got an email from an organization in Germany inviting me to speak at a conference, where they told me the number one Christian publisher in the nation wanted to meet and talk with me about getting my books translated. I flew to Stuttgart, Germany, met the publisher, and now I have six books translated into German. God will put you on the hearts of people in another nation when you start getting clear on your dreams.

This next example is not super spiritual, but I want you to see that God cares about the desires of your heart. I always wanted to write one of my books in an apartment in Paris. When I wrote down that vision, I couldn't afford to take off two or three weeks and go to France to write my next book. But I decided to take God at His Word. I wrote the vision down, and on my vision board I put a photo of a very chic luxury apartment in the City of Light with this scripture: "If you abide in me, and my words abide in you, ask whatever you wish, and it will be done for you" (John 15:7 ESV). Yes, it says that!

Ask whatever you wish?

It is no coincidence that I wrote the book *5 Things Successful People Do Before 8 a.m.* in a Parisian apartment with a view of the Eiffel Tower.

The last example I'll share with you is my dream to teach teenagers how to get a vision and plan for their lives. I went online and googled a bunch of public-school buildings, put them in my dream book, and started asking God to let me teach teenagers how to go after their dreams.

"Whatever you ask in My name, that I will do, that the Father may be glorified in the Son" (John 14:13 NKJV). Is the Father going to be glorified if I can impact teenagers with His Word? Absolutely. Now our Vision Board Course and books are in schools across America, teaching teenagers how to dream big. Start thinking of some big things you need to put on your vision board.

The more vivid you paint a picture of where you want to go, the more decisive you will become! If you sometimes wonder whether it's really that important to mess around with adding pictures to a vision board or book, I am telling you from experience, *it's worth the effort.* I believe that our minds think in pictures, not in words.

Find a photo of your dream house, your ideal body, your perfect vacation. Superimpose your photo on the cover of a book, a magazine, or a newspaper. Get pictures of the bedroom furniture you desire, the wedding ring you love, and the car you'd like to drive. Find photos that match each of your dreams and have fun with this. Instead of always framing your past with the graduation photos, the family vacation from twenty years ago, and the wedding pictures from 1991, why not frame your future? Showcase where you believe God is taking your life.

In 2013 I set a goal to make myself sit quietly for twenty minutes one day per week. Fifty-two times in a year, I sat quietly for twenty minutes and wrote whatever I saw in my spirit about my future. I wrote what I could imagine and visualize happening in my life. I came across that very journal recently, and I began reading some of those private entries. It was verbatim what has happened in my life today! I was seriously stunned to see the accuracy of what I felt God was revealing to me and what my current reality is. The words on those pages and my life today were one and the same.

It's your turn. You will be amazed at what you can accomplish in life when you get crystal clear on what you want.

CHAPTER 14

7 Indicators Successful People Use to Validate Their Dreams

*When God gives you a vision—don't
treat it as a cheap suggestion.*
—MICHAEL TODD

There's a quote that I remember being attributed to Myles Munroe that said, "You can tell when a vision is from God because it makes you look like a fool. And if people believe you the first time you tell them, it's probably not from God." I love how Munroe explained the story of Joseph being in that pit year after year thinking, *This is not what I saw in my dream.* If what you see with your eyes is not what you saw in your heart, it's temporary.

We're going to continue seeing proof of the power of your imagination in the following story, which also sparks the question, How do successful people stay focused on their impossible dreams?

> Gordon was born and raised in the shadow of a shipyard in a little town on the northeast coast of England. Every morning the boy looked out his window as thousands of people went to work, doing the backbreaking labor of building giant vessels that would transport cargo, soldiers, or guests across the world's seas. . . .

Gordon's father wanted his son to become a ship worker. His son had dreams of his own, though, dreams that took him far from the grimy port of his youth. . . . [Gordon] rewrote his father's narrative. Gordon decided that *he* would be the person in the car and that his life's work would take him as far away from Wallsend's shipyard as possible. He pictured an extraordinary life. He would meet kings and queens, presidents, and prime ministers. Millions would know his name. He would travel to exotic places, and he would return home to his own castle.

Those childhood dreams came true for Gordon Sumner, who would later be known by his stage name, "Sting." . . . Sting is one of the world's bestselling artists. In 1977 Sting and his friends formed The Police, a New Wave group that sold more than 75 million albums, making them one of the bestselling bands of all time.[1]

To expound on this radical focus that successful people have, I'm going to share a checklist that I basically stole from my dad's notebook (with his permission) on the seven indicators that your dream is from God.

1. It Captures Your Imagination

"So we fix our eyes not on what is seen, but on what is unseen, since what is seen is temporary, but what is unseen is eternal" (2 Corinthians 4:18). In other words, you dream about it while you're awake. If it's a dream from God, you cannot get it out of your mind. You go to bed thinking, wondering, imagining. You wake up and it's there again.

A beautiful young woman with a thick country accent grew up in the foothills of Tennessee. Her father never learned to read or write, and she was one of twelve children from a very poor family. She would put a tin can on a tobacco stick and jab it into the floor of their old cabin porch. That was her imaginary microphone. The chickens in the yard were her audience. She would imagine her old, ragged clothes were dresses with rhinestones. In her mind she was onstage with her guitar singing to thousands of people.[2]

Dolly Parton used her imagination as a child and then became what she saw.

As you probably know, *Star Wars* is one of the bestselling movies of all time. Other top-grossing films are *E.T.*, *Jurassic Park*, and *Avatar*.[3] Notice each of these films demands that you use your imagination.

> I say, if your knees aren't knocking and your teeth aren't chattering, just a little at least, then you're not playing big enough.
>
> —LISA NICHOLS

Imagination is one of the keys of the most successful dream achievers. It starts with getting quiet and dreaming. God has an assignment for you, and it will require activating your imagination to find out exactly what that mission is.

2. It Seems Impossible

If your dream is possible, you're not dreaming big enough. If it were possible, it wouldn't require faith! The Bible says, "It is impossible to please God without faith" (Hebrews 11:6 NLT). "What is impossible with man is possible with God" (Luke 18:27). God wants us totally dependent on Him.

Kobe Bryant said, "If we have a project and you're saying, 'okay, I can do that,' that's not the project I want. The projects that say, 'I don't know if I can animate that. I don't know how to write that story.' Those are the things we want because through that curiosity you'll reach a level you didn't think was possible."[4]

Here's another example: After growing up in a family with

limited income in Memphis, Tennessee, a young man enlisted with the air force to pursue his dream of becoming a fighter pilot. Once he'd served his four years, he headed to Los Angeles to try a different career: acting.

Sadly, it didn't work out. Next the young man relocated to New York City for another attempt at getting his acting career off the ground, but this time things went so badly that he found himself on the streets and subsisting on stale donuts. Years went by with no success in the industry, but he was able to rent an apartment and find various jobs to pay the bills. He still hadn't given up on his dream, even at age forty-five.

Finally, five years later when he was fifty years old, this man saw his hard work pay off when he began playing bigger roles in popular movies. Today he's an Academy Award winner with a voice that is even more recognizable than his looks: Morgan Freeman, the man who refused to give up on acting, is now one of the most influential actors in Hollywood.[5]

3. It Seems As Though It Will Never Come to Pass

Eileen's early years were filled with sadness. When she was two years old, her parents divorced and she never saw her father again. Her stepfather was violent toward her mother, and many times they were hungry. They lived in a homeless shelter in Toronto, but Eileen had big dreams of being a famous singer.

She started singing in bars when she was only eight years old and remembers her mother waking her up at all hours of the night to get up and perform. The singing brought her a lot of joy, but she detested being surrounded by drunks.

In her late teens and early twenties, it seemed her goal of singing to a more diverse audience was coming true. Then her mother and stepfather were suddenly killed in a head-on car accident. Eileen decided to put her career on hold to step in and take care of her three younger siblings. At twenty-one she became the sole provider for her family. She performed in a local resort until her siblings were old enough to care for themselves.

When many would have given up, Eileen kept her dream alive. It wasn't until her youngest brother graduated from high school that she felt the freedom to head to Nashville and pursue her dream. She changed her name from Eileen Twain to Shania Twain and became one of the highest paid singers in America, winning 223 awards so far![6]

Even though for years it seemed that her dream had to be put on hold and would never come to pass, Shania Twain didn't allow adversity, tragedy, or time to keep her from her destiny—and neither should you. Dale Carnegie agrees: "Most of the important things in the world have been accomplished by people who have kept on trying when there seemed to be no hope at all."[7]

4. Not Everyone Is As Enthusiastic About It As You Are

Did you know that *Star Wars* almost didn't make it to the big screen? There was no money to fund it and at the time—the 1970s—it sounded like a bizarre idea for a movie. But George Lucas had a vision that required staying focused against seemingly insurmountable challenges.[8]

Lucas, a filmmaker, was living in a one-bedroom apartment and struggling to make ends meet. Studio after studio rejected his idea, referring to it as a confusing children's story. Lucas was disappointed but not defeated. Over the years he penned rewrites of rewrites, working hours every day on his script. The story went through count-less changes. In 1976 the final draft was ready. Lucas boarded a flight to Tunisia to start production with an untested cast of new actors and an uninspired crew. A series of accidents and hardships took place—from actors injured on set to equipment breakdowns. A rainstorm struck the country and forced them to leave. The crew offered little resistance as they were not committed to the project.

But Lucas stayed determined and kept moving forward. And that's exactly what you must do even if nobody around you is cheer-ing you on. Lucas admitted to wondering at times if he should just go get a "real" job, but he resolved that he had come too far to quit. "You simply have to put one foot in front of the other and keep going. Put blinders on and plow right ahead."[9] I want you to focus on these words: *you've come too far to quit now!*

On May 25, 1977, *Star Wars* was released in only thirty-two theaters, and to everyone's surprise it broke all box office records. This strange movie that no one had believed in grossed $513 million worldwide. It was named the greatest movie of its time and started a franchise that would attract generations of fans.[10] Lucas said, "If you want to be successful in a particular field, perseverance is one of the key qualities."[11]

5. You Have Experienced Resistance, Difficulty, Setbacks, and Frustration

"Stay with GOD! Take heart. Don't quit. I'll say it again: Stay with GOD" (Psalm 27:14 MSG).

I can't help but think of the grit this guy, Milton, had in pursuing his dream against all odds. Milton dropped out of school in the fourth grade. Later in life he took an apprenticeship with a printing company, only to be fired. That letdown led to him becoming an apprentice to a candymaker. After studying the business for four years, he developed a big vision to start his own candy company and he went for it.

Milton started a candy company in Philadelphia, and, unfortunately, it failed miserably. He picked himself up and went full force after his dream in Chicago. Again it was a devastating failure. Once again he didn't let the severe setbacks stop him. He started another candy company in New York only to watch it go down.

Undeterred, Milton founded the Lancaster Caramel Company. His unique caramel recipe was a huge success; however, Milton believed that chocolate products had a much greater future than caramel. He sold the Lancaster Caramel Company for $1 million in 1900 (that's equivalent to nearly $25 million today) and started a chocolate company called the Hershey Company.[12] Milton Hershey was glued to his vision. And we get to enjoy the sweetness of his persistence!

If Milton had given up on his dreams, we'd probably never know his name. But because he refused to give up against the odds and developed extreme perseverance, his very name is synonymous with chocolate.

If God put a dream in your heart, then He has every intention to help you fulfill it. Your job is to fight against the odds and stay focused on your vision. It's all part of your story that will impact others.

6. It Seems to Consume Your Thinking

Kathryn Stockett's book took five years to get published. Her manuscript brought rejection letter after rejection letter—sixty in total. Despite being told by one publisher that "there's no market for this kind of tiring writing," she refused to give up and kept writing.

Stockett's persistence and work ethic were rewarded when her book was finally published and her words became famous: "You is smart. You is kind. You is important." Kathryn Stockett's book *The*

Help was on the *New York Times* bestsellers list for more than one hundred weeks.[13]

Bottom line: if you can't stop thinking about it, don't stop working toward it. James Allen says, "You are today where your thoughts have brought you; you will be tomorrow where your thoughts take you."

7. It Seems to Define and Shape Your Life

What you're able to do, God wants you to do. Your passion, your potential, and your purpose are all connected. I want you to dream so big and with so much enthusiasm that nobody can talk you out of it.

I heard someone say the saddest day in heaven would be when God gives you a glimpse of all that you could have done, all that you could have been, and all that you could have had, but you let a few setbacks stop you. Don't let that be your story.

CHAPTER 15

Get Your Vision Board in the Right Spot

The tragedy of life doesn't lie in not reaching your goal. The tragedy lies in having no goal to reach. It isn't a calamity to die with dreams unfulfilled, but it is a calamity not to dream.
—DR. BENJAMIN E. MAYS

n 1976 a young Austrian bodybuilder with a thick accent, a name nobody could pronounce, and a box office disappointment under his belt audaciously declared to a sports columnist, "I'm going to be the number one box office star in all of Hollywood."

Arnold Schwarzenegger had the audacity to dream.

Trying not to show doubt or shock over Arnold's big dream, the reporter asked, "How do you plan to become Hollywood's top star?"

"It's the same process I used in bodybuilding. What you do is *create a vision* of who you want to be and then live into that picture as if it were already true." And that's exactly what Schwarzenegger did.[1]

Keeping Dreams Front and Center

I think I've stressed the importance of having a dream and writing it down. Now I want to share the number one reason dreams and goals go unachieved.

Because they're out of sight.

Steve Harvey explained why he is committed to having vision boards: "Man, if I didn't have a vision board, I'd be in trouble. You gotta keep it in front of you. It's on my laptop. It's on my screen on my phone. It's on my iPad. It's on my desktop."[2]

Your life moves toward the images you keep before your eyes.

The Law of Attraction basically states that whatever you focus on, you will attract in your life. Proverbs 23:7 says the same thing: as a man thinks in his heart, so he'll become. When you look at pictures of where you're headed, it gets planted into your subconscious mind, and your subconscious doesn't know any different than to *make that thing happen.*

When Mark Burnett was pitching his idea for the reality show *Survivor,* after being turned down by others in the industry, he handed the president of CBS, Les Moonves, a mock copy of *Newsweek* magazine with a superimposed photo of *Survivor* on the cover.[3] Burnett thinks back to the meeting saying that the pitch worked, and Moonves approved a budget large enough to pay for thirty-nine days of filming in the South China Sea. *Survivor* dominated the ratings and became the number one reality television series of all time.[4]

Images make your dream come alive.

Make Your Dreams Visual

Is it a coincidence that I began realizing my dreams and reaching my goals after I began writing them down, adding pictures to illustrate them, and reviewing them daily? Not one bit. I'm talking about very specific dreams such as:

- Be the keynote speaker at the Amway conference.
- Minister at the largest church in France.
- See my books in the Librairie 7 Ici bookstore in Paris.

- Motivate and minister to the Dallas Cowboys Cheerleaders.
- Have offices on the lake in Rockwall, Texas.
- Get invited to the White House.
- Minister in Moscow, Russia.
- Speak at events with John Maxwell, Ed Mylett, Les Brown, and so many more.

Everything on my vision board years ago is a reality today. I just keep designing new ones. When you design a vision board or even a vision book (place your photos in a spiral notebook or photo album), you are literally surrounding yourself with what can be, not just what is.

We move toward what we *consistently* see. Brian Tracy says, "Perhaps the greatest discovery in human history is this: you become what you think about most of the time."[5]

This powerful principle came from the Word of God: we become what we behold. Your vision for your future needs to be meditated on frequently. *Meditate* means "to think deeply or focus one's mind for a period of time."[6] One meaning of the word *reflect* is synonymous with the definition of *meditate*. An archaic definition of *reflect* means to literally *turn into*.[7] You could say you are "turning into" the images you think of consistently.

It reminds me of the old Polaroid cameras. My daughter bought me one recently for Christmas, a pink one. You simply focus the camera on a subject, click the button, and an image is developed right before your eyes. The point is that whatever you focus on will eventually develop in your life.

You've probably heard, "Keep your goals out of reach but never out of sight." Keep your vision board in a place where you will see it frequently. Be creative and enjoy searching for images that are a tangible representation of where you want your life to go. Your life moves toward the dominating images you keep before your eyes.

Behind-the-Scenes Habits
That Drive Crazy Success

HABIT #5

Look up and use your God-given imagination to create your dream life. Write what you see and keep it before your eyes! It's the alone advantage that leads to living your wildest dreams.

And then God answered, "Write this. Write what you see. Write it out in big block letters so that it can be read on the run."
—HABAKKUK 2:2 MSG

PART 6

Line Up!

CHAPTER 16

What Are You Doing New Year's Eve?

Clarity is the most important single quality of goal setting and perhaps the most important single quality of success.

—BRIAN TRACY

I n an experiment, caterpillars were placed in a circle along the rim of a flowerpot. The lead caterpillar was touching the back of the last one in the circle. The scientist placed a pine needle, which is the food caterpillars thrive on, in the center of the flowerpot. The caterpillars began circling the pine needle and kept going for hours— then for days.

After seven full days, the caterpillars reportedly dropped dead of starvation and exhaustion when their source of nourishment was only six inches away. They were bound to a circle going nowhere.[1] The point is: don't confuse activity with accomplishment. You may be busy but is it moving you toward your destination?

The way we get off the circle is by setting goals that motivate us. Zig Ziglar said, "People complain about a lack of time, but a lack of direction is the real problem."[2] When you set compelling goals, you'll break out of the circle and head for the target.

Don't confuse being busy with being productive. If you feel like your life is constantly on the go but, like the caterpillars, it's not leading you anywhere, then it's time to break the pattern by setting goals.

The Cheerleader of Dreams

I always enjoy getting to meet people at conferences and hear their stories. I stay until the last person leaves because I am a magnet for listening to the dreams in your heart—I'm known as the Cheerleader of Dreams.

A very common thing I hear after I speak is, "Terri, I don't have any dreams." Or "I don't know what my dreams and goals are." And I understand. Because that's exactly where I was in 2002 when I had my wake-up call.

Recently a young mother came up to me and said, "I love this stuff you're talking about, but I have a question for you. My whole life, my dream has always been to get married and have kids, start a family—and I'm doing that! So I've already fulfilled my dreams. What do I do now? I don't have any goals."

I said, "Well, let's think about it. How is your financial condition? Are you enjoying a debt-free life?"

She replied, "Oh my gosh, our finances are a mess."

I said, "Well, there's one goal—actually several—but let's start with one. First, add up all your debt. You need to know where you are financially. Set a goal to pay off the lowest debt you have as soon as possible. Set a deadline to it. It could be to pay off the Visa bill of $2,800 by July 31."

Then I asked, "How is your savings account?"

"We don't have any money saved," she admitted.

I told her that was her second goal to write down: save $1,000. And according to Dave Ramsey, this should be goal number one before you even start paying off debt.

I asked, "What if your car broke down or your kids needed a dentist appointment? You've got to have at least a starting place of $1,000 in emergency money set aside." I suggested having a garage sale, selling some things online, babysitting other people's children, cleaning houses, and so on to earn money to make this emergency fund.

Next I asked about her health and fitness. "Are you where you want to be physically?" She said, "No, I've gained so much weight since I had my kids, and I would love to lose it."

I told her that was goal number three: weigh ___ pounds by April 30.

Finally I asked about her personal growth goals. "You say that being a parent is your greatest ambition and you want to have a strong, healthy family. What are you doing to grow yourself in parenting and being a leader in the family?" I encouraged her to set reading goals in the areas where she needs the most improvement. A good goal would be to read six to twelve books this year. I suggested she find one book on finances and set the goal of reading it in January. I also encouraged her to set other personal growth goals such as enrolling in a course during the first quarter of the year or attending a virtual conference.

I even asked her about the condition of her house. She said, "It's basically a mess at any given time. It looks like someone who has three kids running around lives here, and to be honest, it's a bit stressful." I said, "There's another goal! To make one room as neat and organized as possible and to maintain that neatness every single day for thirty days until it becomes a routine."

She said, "This is so exciting. I have goals!"

Get the picture?

. . .

There's a difference between dreams and goals. As Napoleon Hill says, goals are dreams with a deadline.

Imagine it's New Year's Eve of this upcoming year. You're wearing a festive party hat and "Auld Lang Syne" is playing in the background. Before you blow the party horn and give a kiss to someone special, you reflect over the past twelve months with a smile, and you cheerfully declare, "This has been the most amazing year of my life!"

What would need to happen for you to say that? The answer to that question is how you determine your goals. You project forward, as Brian Tracy teaches,[3] and work backward. Your goals are targets. Without a target, there's nowhere to aim. You need to determine the bullseye to hit this year to feel that it was a successful year. Define what a successful year looks like to you before you begin taking steps toward it.

Sit quietly alone and think. Ask yourself, *How much debt do I want to pay off within the next twelve months? How much money do I want to save over the next year? Where do I want to go on vacation? What do I want my body to look like? What do I want to achieve? How many books do I want to have read? Where do I want to be living, driving, working?*

You need to write down the answers.

I remember hearing a financial expert ask, "If you had no income, no paycheck whatsoever for six months, could you survive? Could you maintain your current lifestyle, pay your bills, and everything go on as normal with no income for six solid months?" That put the fear of God in me. I couldn't even make it until next Friday at that time! I added up my expenses and multiplied the number times six, and that became my financial goal for emergency money.

Got Goals?

In 1997 a guy named Brian Scudamore had a business of hauling off junk and getting paid for it. One day he went away to spend some time alone thinking about his vision, his dreams, and his goals for life. Instead of letting life just keep going by and every year being a repeat of the year before, he went to a place of solitude to think.

Brian took a break to sit on the dock at the family cottage on Bowen Island. Purposing to focus on dreaming instead of on the negatives of his situation, he began writing down his thoughts. "What could the future look like if only I imagined pure possibility?"

This is what he wrote:

1. We would be in the top thirty metros in North America.
2. We would be the FedEx of junk removal. Clean, shiny trucks, friendly uniformed drivers, on time service, upfront rates.[4]

Once Brian made the vision clear and started setting specific goals, ideas began to emerge. He started brainstorming his venture when "Got milk?" was enjoying success. 1–800-GOT-JUNK? became his new business name.

He signed fifty-three franchise deals that one year! Today, his company is in every major city in the United States, Canada, and Australia with a revenue of a quarter billion dollars—hauling off junk![5]

CHAPTER 17

7 Tips Successful People Use to Set Goals

*If you plan to excel in big things, you have to
develop the habit in the small ones.*
—LECRAE

W ho would've ever dreamed years ago that the guy dressed in a chicken costume waving your car down in front of a fast-food restaurant would become the Oscar-winning actor Brad Pitt? Or that the peanut vendor at the Oakland A's baseball stadium would one day be one of the highest-paid actors in Hollywood, Tom Hanks? Or that the girl scooping thirty-one flavors of ice cream at Baskin-Robbins would become *Pretty Woman* star Julia Roberts?[1] Small beginnings are simply stepping stones to a brighter future.

Everybody wants the big success—the big house, the big business, the big income. There's nothing wrong with wanting to do big things, but we must remember that greatness starts off small. Goals are the stepping stones on the way to your big dreams.

In light of the importance of taking steps to turn those dreams into reality, here are seven tips for how to set goals:

1. Set Seven to Ten Goals for the Year

In my experience, setting between seven and ten goals is the most effective. When we have too many goals, we lose our focus and don't achieve any of them. There's an old phrase that says, "If you aim at too many targets, you miss all of them."

2. Write Them Down in the *Present Tense*

Writing down your dreams and goals is a clear key to success. Why do successful people write everything down? From dreams and goals to self-discovery and daily to-do lists, they write things down because if they don't, they'll forget. It's as simple as it sounds.

When you put something in writing, it instantly proves you're serious. Whether it's the chore of doing laundry Saturday morning or the goal of writing a book before the year ends, after it's written down it becomes concrete, and your chance of following through goes up 42 percent![2]

A well-known study by Virginia Tech professor Dr. David Kohl proved the power of the pencil when he asked random people on the street one question: "What are your goals for life?" An alarming 80 percent responded that they had no goals. Sixteen percent said they had goals but not written down. Ultimately only 3 percent had written down goals, with just 1 percent reviewing what they wrote.[3]

Even the weight loss industry found that those who keep a food journal are more successful at losing weight and keeping it off than those who don't write down what they eat. It's easy to overlook the dips into the candy stash at the office or that second trip to the buffet line if we're not confronted with seeing what we chose to eat on paper. They say, "If you bite it, write it."

3. Be Very Specific

According to statistics, about 25–40 percent of Americans make New Year's resolutions, yet only 9 percent are successful in achieving their goals.[4] In fact, we tend to set the same goals many times with no success. See if you can relate to these most popular resolutions compiled by Brad Zomick:[5]

- Exercise more
- Get organized
- Learn a new skill or hobby
- Spend less money
- Read more
- Travel more
- Get closer to God

That's exactly how I used to set goals year after year—and never achieve them. Until I learned this private habit of the most successful people in the world. The problem with these goals and the reason they go unachieved year after year is that they're too vague. Vague goals produce vague results. Get crystal clear by being very specific, such as:

- Our Visa bill of $9,456.12 is paid off by March 10.
- My student loan of $11,000 is completely paid in full by July 31.
- Enjoy a weekend getaway to New York City for $3,000 by April 15.
- Sell five houses by September 30.
- Successfully save $5,000 by December 31.
- Finish my manuscript and have it ready to be printed by June 30.
- Read twelve books by December 31.

4. Establish Deadlines

As you can see in the examples above, every goal needs a deadline. Why? Because deadlines are motivating. They create a sense of urgency. The best way to get your house cleaned up is to invite company over! Why? There's a deadline.

If you have the desire to write a book, you need to assign a deadline for chapter 1. Don't just set a goal of "write my book this year." Make it specific, such as "write chapter 1 by March 31."

5. Stretch Out of Your Comfort Zone

If all your goals are in your comfort zone, they won't challenge you. This doesn't require you to think creatively, to pray, to learn anything new, or to put a demand on your faith to grow. And that's not going to motivate you.

One way I've learned to set a specific goal is by asking myself a simple question: What's the coolest thing that could happen this year?

It's exciting to set a goal so big that you can't achieve it until you grow into the person who is capable of it. You will feel doubt, fear, awkwardness, and anxiety, but that just means you're being stretched! It means that you'll need to grow to reach these goals.

A personal example: Years ago I got too comfortable hosting my women's conference, ICING, at a certain venue. We had held the event at a coliseum in Fort Worth for several years. In the beginning that was a major stretch, but we got comfortable. We could almost do this conference in our sleep. One year we decided to take a huge step of faith and rent the Toyota Music Factory in Dallas, Texas. To put this in perspective, our budget more than doubled! That's uncomfortable. We changed so many things: the location, the time of year, the price to attend, the music—everything was scary.

Talk about goals that make your knees knock and your teeth chatter—this was one for me! But I've discovered that God loves nothing more than to see His children use their faith for big goals and trust Him to make it possible. The Tuesday before the event started on Friday, our venue was completely paid in full—with a budget that had doubled. God responds to great faith!

6. Make Your Goals Visible and Declare Them All Year Long

We covered this point in the last section with vision boards, but as a reminder, this is one of the biggest reasons goals are not achieved. We tend to stick them in a drawer, we put them on the computer but never go back to look at them, we leave them filed away in a three-ring binder that we never refer to again. That used to be me. I would put them in my nightstand and not revisit them until New Year's Eve to see if anything had magically happened!

Today in the office hallway we have a giant vision board with our top ten goals for the year for the entire team to see consistently. We get the goals out at our team meetings and read them out loud one by one. (I'll explain in part 6 the importance of making positive declarations.)

If you keep your goals visible, when December rolls around you're not surprised. When you practice these tips, you will know exactly how you're tracking all year long.

7. Set Three Milestones for Each Goal

You've probably heard the old saying about how to eat an elephant: one bite at a time. A goal must be broken down into thin slices. Many times we set big, lofty goals and immediately we're stressed out. Your goals should stretch you, not stress you. You need to break down each goal into bite-size pieces.

For example, let's say you set a goal to gain 1,000 subscribers to your YouTube channel by December 31. That number looks overwhelming, especially if you have 135 subscribers right now. Next, you establish three major milestones on the way to that big goal.

> 1st milestone: 300 subscribers (That means you more than doubled! Make a big deal about it.)
> 2nd milestone: 500 subscribers (Again, celebrate that major win and keep going.)
> 3rd milestone: 750 subscribers (This is incredible! Throw a party!)
> Big goal: 1,000 subscribers (You did it!)

You will focus more on the milestones, which doesn't stress you out, and stay motivated to strive for the big goal. This lets you know you're on the right path. You're going in the right direction.

You can do this with financial goals— eliminating debt, saving money, growing your investments—weight-loss goals, personal growth goals, and so forth.

It's kind of like when you're on a plane flying overseas and you watch that large map of the world with the little tracker showing your flight. As time goes by, you can see the little plane on the screen make its way across the entire United States and across the Pacific Ocean. This is a visual reminder of how much progress you are making. It's the same way with setting milestones on the way to achieving your big goals.

There is an old saying that goes, "By the yard it's hard; but inch by inch, anything's a cinch."

The Thirty-Day Challenge

Brian Tracy recommends something I've done for years: write down your top ten goals in a notebook for thirty days without skipping a day *and* without looking back to the previous day to see what you wrote. In other words, if you can't remember all ten on day two, it's okay. Perhaps all ten weren't that important to you, so just write what you remember and do this for a full month.

This daily practice will cause your goals to become so ingrained in your subconscious mind that you become more determined than ever to go after them and then enjoy the thrill of checking them off.[6]

Why Bother?!

Years ago, my dad and I were at Dallas/Fort Worth International Airport on our way to a conference, and he wanted to stop by Starbucks. He ordered a low-fat decaf coffee with 2 percent milk and no whipped cream.

The cashier yelled his order to the barista: "One medium Why Bother!"

"What did you call it?" my dad said.

"A cup of Why Bother," she answered. In other words, what's the point in getting coffee when you're leaving out all the good stuff?

We tend to feel the same way when we launch new success habits. Why bother listening to a message on my way to work? Why bother cutting out one hour of television each night to read? Why bother writing down my goals for thirty days? Why even bother making a vision board?

In the beginning all your efforts will feel insignificant—why bother? Plus, nobody sees all the effort you're extending, as it's all behind closed doors.

The most successful people in the world bother! Every day matters. Every inch of progress is still progress. In 2002, when I began these little habits of personal development in private, I never dreamed I would still be practicing them today and sharing them with you. In addition, I never imagined what a monumental change they would produce in my life and, ultimately, enable me to live my dreams.

Again, what's simple to do is also simple not to do. The biggest difference in dreamers and dream-achievers is that those who achieve their aspirations are willing to do what others are not willing to do. I can't help but think how most people don't see me Monday morning at five o'clock, rolling out of bed, slipping on my jogging clothes, going outside in the dark to drive to the gym, lift weights, walk on the treadmill, and listen to messages for a full hour. They don't see me return home, go into my home office, sit on my chaise lounge, spend time in prayer, pray over my vision board, write down my goals, worship God, shower, get dressed, and go to work.

People may scroll through my Instagram or Facebook page and think, *Wow! She does book signings in Paris, France! She's on television. She just launched another new book. She speaks to thousands of people.* My response is that the secret of your future is always hidden in your daily routine.

When Dr. Bell asked a study group of four thousand retired executives with an average age of seventy, "If you could live your life over again, what would you do differently?" the most common response was, "I should have taken charge of my life and set my goals earlier."[7]

Change your routine, and you can change your life. Bother with these habits because little by little adds up to a lot.

CHAPTER 18

Get Comfortable Saying No

Focusing is about saying no.
—STEVE JOBS

When Warren Buffett was asked to summarize his key to success, his shocking response was that he says no to almost everything.[1] Think about that. Buffett attributes his unprecedented success to his ability to say no in order to stay focused on what he's saying yes to. Let me explain.

The late Steve Jobs was asked, "What are you most proud of in terms of breakthrough products that you and Apple have built?" Jobs said, "I am as proud of what we don't do as I am of what we do. Deciding what not to do is just as important as what to do."[2] That statement is true for companies, entrepreneurs, stay-at-home moms, and real estate agents—for everyone.

If you are committed to achieving the dreams and goals in your heart, you must get comfortable saying no to anything that stops your progress, fights for your attention, and distracts you. I love the statement, "Decide what your priorities are and how much time you'll spend on them. If you don't, someone else will."

■ ■ ■

When lion tamers were asked why they always carry a four-legged stool into the cage with a wild animal, along with a pistol and a whip, they replied that the stool is the most important in their defense. They always hold the stool by the seat and thrust the four legs toward the face of the lion. This is an intentional tactic to force the lion to focus on all four legs of the stool at once. Doing this causes the lion's attention to be fragmented. The lion's attention is all over the place trying to focus on four things, and, as a result, the lion becomes paralyzed with overwhelm.[3]

The same can happen to us. When our attention is all over the place, we're focusing on too many goals, we say yes to too many opportunities, and our to-do list has thirty-four items, we become tame, weak, and unable to achieve our most important goals.

Focus is the opposite of being distracted. When we have too many ideas and opportunities, we lose our focus and end up accomplishing nothing. Success is determined just as much by what we say no to as what we say yes to. Instead of making a to-do list, start making a to-don't list and identify what you can start saying no to today.

Dave Ramsey made the same point:

> My grandmother says, "Baby, if you want your *yes* to have any value, you have to become more comfortable with your *no.*"
> —LISA NICHOLS

There's a power to focus. If you don't focus on something, nothing gets done. Money is the same way. When you try to focus on sixteen things at once, nothing happens. . . . We are so crazy that we say stop doing anything with money except paying your minimum payments. Stop your 401K (temporarily), stop saving (temporarily), stop paying an extra $30 on that debt, and let's do one thing at a time and totally focus our energy on that! And then progressively move on.[4]

John Maxwell said,

I tend to want to do everything. If one is good, four is better. I love saying yes. I have a very hard time saying no. As a result, I get spread too thin. To deal with that, I had to develop a system. I was no longer allowed to answer requests for my time. Instead, requests had to go to a group who would decide whether I would accept a speaking engagement or other request. We call them the Hatchet Committee because they put the ax to 90 percent of the requests that came in. It was the only system that I could find that forced me to maintain my priorities when it came to my time.[5]

And he's written more than one hundred books, selling a total of more than 30 million copies! What do you need to say no to so you can stay focused on your most important goals?

- You want to be debt-free? Say no to the extravagant vacation this year.
- You want to write a book? Say no to going to the mall with your friends Saturday morning so you have that time to write.
- You want to be in the best shape of your life? Say no to the quick drive-thru restaurant to fill up on junk.
- You want to grow in your personal development? Say no to watching four hours of television each day.
- You want to develop success habits? Say no to sleeping that extra thirty minutes each morning.

Behind-the-Scenes Habits
That Drive Crazy Success

HABIT #6

Line up your top-ten goals in writing by pretending it's a future New Year's Eve and you just enjoyed the greatest year you've ever had. It's the alone advantage that leads to being a lifelong goal-setter.

I press on toward the goal to win the prize for which God has called me heavenward in Christ Jesus.
—PHILIPPIANS 3:14

PART 7

Speak Up!

CHAPTER 19

Be Your Own Cheerleader

Your words have the power to hurt, to heal, open minds, open hearts and change the world. Never forget the responsibility you have over the words you speak.
—STEVEN AITCHISON

S elena Gomez has more Instagram followers than any other woman in the world.[1] While she may be popular, she's not a stranger to severe setbacks and difficulties. Raised by a single mom struggling financially, Selena was diagnosed with the autoimmune disease lupus and underwent chemotherapy. The disease caused serious complications that led to a kidney transplant. After recovering, Gomez opened up about her long-lasting battle with depression and anxiety.[2]

Before and after performing on stage, Gomez would have severe panic attacks. Depression and anxiety were a part of her life for five years straight. It wasn't enough to just listen to a motivational message—she needed more intentional action. In addition to counseling, Selena began using positive affirmations to begin each day, such as, "I am enough."[3]

What do successful people do in private so they're rewarded in public? They make positive declarations over themselves. They prophesy their future. They declare their destiny with nobody around.

Your words matter. Your internal and external conversation with yourself either supports or undermines your progress toward your goals. You may not even be aware of the things you're saying to yourself because you've been saying them for so long.

Steve Harvey said,

We have to be aware of the conversation we are having with ourselves. What are you saying to yourself when no one else is around? What are the conversations that you are having in the mirror with yourself each morning? Are you speaking life into your dreams, or are you repeating someone else's fears and anxieties? Are you front-loading your day with Scriptures, affirmations, and positive quotations, or are you dumping doubt and anguish into your spirit?

And then Harvey made this eye-opening statement: "You think that you're the only one who can see your words of defeat, but they show up in your demeanor and how you present yourself to the world."[4]

Years ago, before my fitness trainer gave me a workout plan, she said, "Let's work on your self-image, starting with your posture."

I was like, "What? I want to work on my thighs."

She said, "I want you to pull your shoulders back and carry yourself with more confidence. I want you to sit in your car with excellent posture and adjust the rearview mirror to your new position. If suddenly you can't see what's behind you, don't adjust the mirror—adjust you. Your self-image can be seen in your posture."

It wasn't until 2007 that I sat down with my journal and made a list of positive declarations to speak over myself. Nearly every word on those pages was the exact opposite of who I was at the time, but I was establishing a new identity. I wrote things such as "I am confident" (I was riddled with insecurity), "I am courageous" (I was extremely timid and scared), and "I am qualified by God" (I felt so unprepared for the big dreams in my heart).

Who do you need to become to live out the dreams in your heart? For a moment, imagine the best version of yourself—the version of you who has everything on your vision board. Decide the identity you want to have.

When God puts a dream in your heart, you have to decide to be your own cheerleader. We have enough critics in the world; stop being critical of yourself. That's what a red-haired, blue-eyed young British boy with a stuttering problem did when the odds were against him. Not only was Ed Sheeran bullied as a kid, but he also battled enormous insecurities due to a lazy eye and speech problems—side effects of a surgery necessary to save his vision.[5]

He overcame the stuttering challenge by mimicking famous rappers on the radio and began writing his own music.[6] Facing difficulty after difficulty, he decided to take a bold step by posting a video of himself playing his music online. Little by little, he began to get noticed by influential people. He admits to being petrified, but he overcame his insecurities and went for his dream. By 2011 his debut album topped the charts in the UK.[7]

. . .

In his bestselling book *Atomic Habits,* James Clear tells the story of two people resisting an offered cigarette. One person says, "No thanks. I'm trying to quit." This person still identified as a smoker trying to be someone they weren't. "They are hoping their behavior will change while carrying around the same beliefs," Clear explains. "The second person declines by saying, 'No thanks. I'm not a smoker.'" The wording differences were minor, but the mindset change was major. The second person had already decided smoking was their past, not their present.[8]

Once you've decided on a shift in your identity, you will begin walking in alignment with that new self-image. So how you see yourself is how you will act. If you view yourself as undisciplined, you will maintain an undisciplined lifestyle.

I heard a true story about a young guy who was rebellious, hung out with the wrong crowd, and skipped school all the time, clearly headed down the wrong path. At his mother's pleading, he agreed to at least see if he could be accepted to college, which meant taking the SAT. About a month after taking the test, his score came in the mail and shocked him: 1480 out of 1600. (Um, that's incredible. I speak from someone who did not score nearly that high.)

His mother actually asked if he had cheated, and his response was, "I tried to cheat, but the way the seats were arranged, I couldn't see."

The young man was now entering his senior year of high school, and the high score urged him to a decision. "Wow, if I'm really that smart, I might as well go to class." This change in his lifestyle meant his social circles changed, and even his teachers began to respond to him more positively. He graduated, was accepted at an Ivy League school, got an MBA, and attained great success.

It took more than a decade for the SAT board to realize their mistake. One day the man opened a letter that informed him the test score he'd received was a mistake. Instead of earning a 1480, he'd made a 740.

He said, "Most people think the 1480 is what changed my life, but what changed my life was when I started acting like a 1480. I asked myself what does a 1480 do? And I started doing it."[9]

Who do you need to become to achieve your goals? Once you decide your new identity, don't stop there. Affirm it with your words every day. Job 22:28 says, "Thou shalt also decree a thing, and it shall be established unto thee" (KJV). Maybe you have stayed in a rut—hopeless, bored, and undisciplined—because you've been saying negative things about yourself. So start speaking the opposite.

Did you know that while the first pencils were in use by the early seventeenth century, the eraser was only invented (unintentionally!)

almost 150 years later?[10] I'm so grateful erasers exist, because I've erased more in my life than I've kept, including erasing a poor self-image.

It's time to change by making positive declarations over yourself. You must become your own cheerleader with the words of your mouth behind closed doors. The Bible says, "David *encouraged himself* in the LORD his God" (1 Samuel 30:6 KJV). You have to keep yourself encouraged. If you want to see where your life is headed, listen to the words that are coming out of your mouth.

■ ■ ■

Do you feel like the dream in your heart is hopeless? Ezekiel 37 tells of a man who faced a dead, barren situation, helpless to make any changes on his own—a literal valley of dead bones. God set Ezekiel down in the middle of them and asked him, "Can these bones live?" (verse 3). Picture this in your mind. There was no sign of life. It was all dead. He was looking at it and saw the proof. Nothing was happening. It was over.

Think about that in reference to your dreams. Sometimes there are so many negatives around us that it feels like there is no hope to be found. Hope appears dead. It's over. God is asking you today what he asked Ezekiel: "Can these bones live?" In other words, "Can this barren, dried-up dream still live?" Can this dried-up marriage still make it? Can this barren body still have children? Can this invisible savings account still grow?

But God gave Ezekiel the secret to resurrecting a dead dream: *speak life.* Notice the solution to giving life to death is in the words of your mouth. Verse 7 says, "So I prophesied as I was commanded. And as I was prophesying, there was a noise, a rattling sound, and the bones came together, bone to bone." God gave them life again. And He will do the same for your dreams, but you must speak to them. The dreams in your heart come to life by speaking words of life over them.

What are you saying about your life? Your finances? Your family? Your health? Your career? Your very own words shape your world.

- "I'll never live in a house like that!"
- "I'll never have that kind of salary!"
- "I'm always sick."
- "I just have a slow metabolism."
- "I'll never get promoted at this rate!"
- "I've reached my limits."
- "I'm not qualified."
- "I'm too afraid to step out and do something different."
- "I'll always be in debt!"
- "No matter what I try, I can't lose weight!"
- "I could never be friends with them."
- "I'm too shy."

Becoming your own cheerleader is a two-step process: stop speaking negatively and start speaking positively. It's not okay to be overly critical of yourself. Start taking an inventory of what you're allowing to roll off your tongue. Ask yourself, "Is what I'm about to say what I want to come about in my life?" If it does not line up with your dreams and your new identity, then don't voice it.

In the book of Luke, an angel appeared to Zechariah, informing him that he was going to have a baby and instructing him to name the baby John. Overcome with doubt, Zechariah responded with unbelief, "Are you sure? Do you know how old I am?"

Are you responding with the same negativity because of your current age? Are you questioning the dreams in your heart because you feel you're too old, too young, or too beyond the perfect time to seize opportunities?

Let's see how the angel responded to those negative words. He said, "Because you doubted, you will remain silent and not speak until the baby is born" (Luke 1:20, my paraphrase). Think about that—for nine solid months Zechariah could not speak. That's how detrimental our words are over our future.

Stop speaking negative, devastating, failure-driven words out of your mouth, and start proactively speaking positive, faith-filled, success-driven words! Like the Lord told Joyce Meyer, "It's one thing to stop saying the wrong things, but you've got to start saying the right things."[11]

I must be honest: the first few times I did this all by myself, I felt like a nut. My husband was upstairs playing video games, my daughter was in her playroom watching a movie, and I went into our guest bedroom with my handwritten notebook of declarations. I stood there in the silence and just began speaking them out one by one, hoping my family wasn't standing in the hall listening to me.

- "I am proactive."
- "I am in the best shape of my life."
- "I am bold and courageous."
- "I am a voice impacting France for Jesus."
- "I am confident to minister on television."
- "I am confident to minister to thousands of people."
- "I speak at the largest conferences in the world."

When I began this *demonstration of faith*, I had never ministered in the nation of France—ever! And the largest crowd I had ever spoken to was probably about three hundred people. However, each morning before I would jump in my car and go to the office, I would go into our guest bedroom, grab that little (life-changing) list of declarations, and speak them by faith! Morning after morning, sunrise after sunrise, month after month.

I'll never forget the evening of March 12, 2012, as I stood on the front row of the largest church in the nation of France and prepared to take the stage. My daughter leaned over to me and asked, "Mama, are you a little nervous?" Rightfully so, as I was preparing to minister to approximately ten thousand people in Paris. I answered, "I am confident to minister to thousands of people. I speak at the largest conferences in the world."

Why would I reply so courageously? Because what you repeatedly hear, you eventually believe! And you believe yourself more than anyone else. If you want to know where your life is headed, listen to the words coming out of your mouth. I will never regret those morning routines alone, in the quietness of that little guest bedroom in Burleson, Texas, because they have enabled me to stand on stages to minister at some of the largest conferences in the world.

If you only knew how many times I have walked into a local bookstore, pointed to the shelves, and declared (by faith), "My books are sold on these bookshelves in Jesus' name!" As you can imagine, my books are now sold in those bookstores. Or how many times I have declared that "my gift is making room for me and bringing me before great men." I have even superimposed a photo of John Maxwell with one of me (a totally fake picture) and one of Ed Mylett and me. But today I speak at events with John Maxwell and Ed Mylett. There's power in your words!

It's time for you to learn this "foreign" language. This language of success. It is the language of God in which you no longer speak of the problem, you speak of the solution. Literally, you prophesy your future. You proactively go after your dreams with the words of your mouth. Whatever you want to see happen in your life, speak it out in faith in the privacy of your bedroom, kitchen, car, shower, wherever you are.

CHAPTER 20

The 5 *Ps* Successful People Practice

If you want to be successful, the first thing
you need to do is get serious.
—JIM ROHN

L isa Nichols, who I wrote about in chapter 3, was in an abusive, violent relationship. When she finally mustered the courage to get out of that relationship, Lisa said, "I was just different."

Her mom insisted that she visit a doctor to get some treatment. As she sat on the table waiting for the diagnosis, the doctor walked in and said carefully, "Lisa, you're clinically depressed."

What? "I read the prescription and it said 'Prozac' with my name on it," said Lisa. "That doesn't make sense."

She asked the doctor, "Do you mean I'm sad?"

"Very, very sad."

"Doctor, can I try something?"

Her doctor agreed but made her commit to returning within thirty days.

Lisa said she went home and did three things. First, every day she got in front of her mirror and drilled the words *I am!*

I am strong.
I am confident.

I am secure.

I am capable.

I am victorious.

I am an overcomer.

I am made in the image of God.

I am highly favored of God.

I am beautiful.

I am anointed.

Every single day!

Lisa said she had forgotten who she was. She covered her home in affirmations to help remind her of the truth about herself. She also was diligently reading Scripture and seeking to deal with the guilt, shame, and trauma of her experiences.

Thirty days later, Lisa returned for her scheduled appointment and she was on fire. She was a completely different person! After extensive questioning, her doctor asked, "What have you been doing? Can I use it with other patients?"[1]

(Just a quick note to say that while Lisa's story is inspiring, it's not intended to imply that medication is never needed in treatment.)

When you embrace this private key to success, I want you to picture an old record being scratched. Something is scratching it so hard that it can't ever be played again. It's a broken record. It's useless. The more you speak positive declarations and proclaim God's Word over yourself, the more a new record is being played in your head.

Remember, *your* voice is the most influential voice in your life. Whatever you put after the words *I am* becomes your reality. Let's look at a few tips to help you get started making the right kind of declarations—the five *P*s successful people practice.

1. Positive

It's so important that you avoid negative statements when you make your declarations. Refrain from using words such as *no, not, never, don't, can't, lose, quit, stop,* and *avoid.* Remember this key phrase: *focus on what you do want, not on what you don't want.*

Your words create mental images in your mind, and when you focus on the negative, you are focusing on the very thing you don't want. For example, it's not as effective to declare, "I'm not overweight. I am losing weight." You are affirming what you're trying to get rid of. Declare the ideal weight you want to have rather than how many pounds you want to lose: "I am at a healthy weight of ____ for my body." That's a positive declaration of faith.

"Am I telling the truth, Terri, when I make these statements?"

I understand the question and speculation about whether you're just making up false statements that are contrary to your reality. But you are simply speaking the way God speaks. Look at this translation of Romans 4:17: "[God] gives life to the dead and speaks of the *nonexistent* things . . . as if they [already] existed" (AMPC).

2. Personal

When you personalize your declarations and scriptures from God's Word as written straight to you, they are directed right to your life. God loves nothing more than to hear His children take His Word personally and then speak it back to Him.

Make it personal to your situation. It may include adopting a baby, learning a foreign language, acquiring a new skill, living in a certain city, and so on. Make it personal to your life.

In my book *Pep Talk,* I dedicated an entire chapter to making positive declarations over your dreams and goals. I am absolutely convinced that getting clear on your dreams and writing them down are vital keys to success, but that's not enough. What's coming out of your mouth has everything to do with what you are experiencing. For example, my personal dreams included the following.

- A photo taken of Joyce Meyer's women's conference in a coliseum (taken from her website). I put my head on top of hers (don't laugh) with the declaration, "I speak to thousands of people" (which I had never done).
- A map of France with the declaration, "My books are translated into French" (when I didn't have or even know of any French publishers).
- A photo of the Dallas Cowboys Cheerleaders (no, I'm not still dreaming of being a professional cheerleader for the NFL at my age). Instead of being a cheerleader, I declared, "I minister to the Dallas Cowboys Cheerleaders."

These are just a few of the dreams I pinned on my vision board and consistently declared verbally. Every dream I just shared with you has been fulfilled, as have many more. Why? Your words create your world. Your life moves toward the words you speak.

3. Present Tense

Many times we are prone to making positive declarations about ourselves in the future. We make the mistake of thinking this is something that will happen much later. When we make statements such as, "I will make more money" or "I will get that new job" or "I will have a baby," it places our faith on the thought that one day, someday, just beyond reach, but not now!

We serve the Great I AM, not the great I WILL BE! I highly encourage you to begin many of your declarations with "I am—" For example, I am healthy. I am a bestselling author. I am beautiful inside and out. I am confident. I am full of courage. I am on time everywhere I go. I am an excellent leader.

4. Precise

We've already discussed how vague goals produce vague results, but it's also true with declarations when it comes to the *personal* dreams and goals you have for your life. Yes, you need to make declarations such as: "I am healthy. I am energetic. I am enthusiastic about my life." Additionally, the more accurate you are with your personal dreams and goals, the better the outcome. Doing this gives you a clear mental picture to focus on.

Another one of my precise declarations is that *I am an expert in the message that God has given me to share.* I have confessed that for years, countless times. But I'll never forget the first time I did a television interview being aired across the globe. Seconds before we went live, the audio engineer was adjusting my mic and quickly said, "Terri, sit over there in the expert chair." I snickered inside to myself, *Expert chair? What am I an expert in?* And then it dawned on me, "Oh my goodness! I've been declaring for years that *I am an expert in the message God has given me to share.* It's happening!"

5. Passionate

The more emotion you have behind your declaration, the more effective it will be. When you simply go down a list of sentences reciting them in a robotic tone because I recommended you do this to succeed, you can forget it. There's no passion, no enthusiasm, and no faith behind it.

For example, I have declared for years that *I am a bestselling author, and I am signing a book deal with the best publisher in the world*. Years ago, a friend of mine arranged a phone call for me with one of the biggest book agents in America. I was reluctant to agree to this call, though I've always prayed for God to open doors for me and to give me His favor in unprecedented ways. And He always has. However, I also know that to go to a new level, you have to get out of your comfort zone. So I pushed myself out.

I had the phone call, and I tried my best to sell myself (which I loathe) and prove to this agent that she should sign me, and I would do my best to sell a ton of books. Well, in a very deep, sort of sultry voice she said, "You are adorable" (referring to my childlike voice). But that was about it.

Being adorable doesn't get a book deal.

But I kept declaring with passion that *I am a bestselling author, and I am signing with the best publisher in the world!* I even act as if it's already happened. I've been known to jump and squeal and announce it to my friends so convincingly that they respond, "You did?"

Seven years after that *adorable* phone call—I repeat, *seven* years—I signed with a different agent. Minutes after that contract was emailed to me, my agent sent me this text: "I don't know if signing a book deal with the largest Christian publisher in the world was on your vision board, but you just did."

As a matter of fact—ha!

I believe your passion, your strong belief in God's ability to bring what you're declaring, touches the heart of God! When He sees that you wholeheartedly believe in what you're saying, He sends angels to go to work on your behalf and make your declarations a reality!

The angels are listening. They are on standby just waiting to hear you speak faith-filled words so they can carry them out. Isn't that amazing? You may or may not find this hard to believe, but I can prove it from God's Word. Psalm 103:20 says, "Bless the LORD, ye his angels, that excel in strength, that do his commandments, *hearkening unto the voice of his word*" (KJV).

How do you activate angels on your behalf? This verse reveals that angels "hearken" (or "listen, giving respectful attention") unto the voice of the Lord—unto His Word. Angels still do this today. God gives instructions to His angels, and they carry them out. I believe that when we speak God's Word, we release our angels to go to work on our behalf. However, when we speak contrary to the Word of God, we prevent our angels from benefiting our lives.

I also believe that when you speak God's Word, you have the ear of Almighty God. When you speak the name of Jesus, all heaven stands at attention.

Blow the Whistle

Have you ever watched a professional football game and noticed that man with a black-and-white-striped shirt on, with a whistle around his neck? He may appear small in stature compared to the 350-pound lineman he's officiating, but when he blows his whistle, that mammoth football player comes to a screeching halt. How does this referee have such power over this herd of seeming giants? It's because the moment the man in the black-and-white-striped shirt blows that whistle, those enormous men in football pads know that all the NFL is backing him up!

That's exactly what happens in your life when you call on the name of Jesus to help you achieve your impossible dreams. You're not trying to succeed in your own strength. You now have all of heaven backing you up!

You don't have to force the right doors to open for you, manipulate things to get around the right people, or try to be successful in your own power. You can call on heaven to do for you what you could never do on your own. Just blow the whistle. What does that mean? Call on Jesus to help you. He's the one who said, "[I] will not fail thee nor forsake thee" (Deuteronomy 31:6 KJV). And He meant it.

We tend to think God would never open doors for us, favor us, or give us special advantages. Did you know that one of the definitions of the "favor of God" is "disposed to show preferential treatment"?

"Oh, Lord GOD! Behold, You Yourself have made the heavens and the earth by Your great power and by Your outstretched arm! Nothing is too difficult for You" (Jeremiah 32:17 NASB). You're not bothering God when you call on Him. You're not inconveniencing Him when you ask Him for good breaks, favorable opportunities, and divine connections. You are His child, and He is standing by, waiting for you to blow the whistle so heaven can back you up and do for you what you could never do on your own.

You don't want your angels to be bored all day, do you? Blow the whistle!

CHAPTER 21

Get Your Megaphone Ready

Everything I set my hands to prospers and succeeds.
—DEUTERONOMY 28:8 (AUTHOR PARAPHRASE)

A short film (that's gone viral on YouTube) tells the story of a man who is blind sitting on the pavement in front of a government building. He's holding a homemade sign that reads, "I'm blind. Please help." Most people continue about their business and hastily pass by the man without much notice, and he receives just a few measly donations.

Suddenly, a young professional woman stops and stands in front of him. The man reaches down to feel her shoes to get some sort of idea of who is standing before him. She bends down, picks up his sign, flips it over, and begins to write. Afterward, she places the sign back in his hands and leaves. But something remarkable begins to happen. People stop, they read the sign, and they leave money.

Later the young professional returns and notices a crowd of people by the man, making considerable donations. When she approaches, he reaches down and recognizes the feel of her shoes. He curiously asks, "Miss, please tell me. What did you write on my sign?"

She says, "Just the same thing you wrote. I just used different words." The camera then zooms in on the man's sign that reads, "It's a beautiful day, but I can't see it." The video ends with this powerful declaration: "Change your words, change your world."[1]

Change Your Words, Change Your World

Just as a simple change of words changed the man's outcome, the same can happen for you. I have provided some samples of declarations and personalized scriptures to get you started down the road of success. So get your megaphone ready and start your declarations.

I declare in the name of Jesus:
I am highly favored of God.
I am accomplishing everything God has placed in my heart
    to do.
I have the grace of God to help me accomplish my dreams.
I am highly proactive.
I am courageous in the pursuit of my dreams.
I am sensitive to God's timing in my life.
I take bold steps of faith.
I am expecting breakthroughs in my life.
I expect blessings to chase me down and overtake me.
I am faithful to God, and He is faithful to me.
God is restoring the years that were stolen from me.
I am always in the right place at the right time.
I have extraordinary opportunities given to me.
I have preferential treatment because of God's favor.
I receive solutions to every problem, challenge, and obstacle.
I am fulfilling my destiny.
I embrace every new season God has for me.
I am thriving in life.
I pray with boldness and confidence.
I am programmed for success.
I live with purpose and passion.
I am a person of excellence and integrity.
I am fulfilling my life assignment down to the last detail.

Personalized Scriptures to Declare

I will be strong and not give up, for my work will be rewarded.
(2 Chronicles 15:7)

God is giving me the desires of my heart and making all my
plans succeed. (Psalm 20:4)

I delight myself in the Lord, and He will give me the desires of
my heart. (Psalm 37:4)

I trust in the Lord with all my heart and lean not on my own
understanding. In all my ways I acknowledge Him, and He
shall direct my path. (Proverbs 3:5–6)

I commit to the Lord whatever I do, and He will establish my
plans. (Proverbs 16:3)

I do not remember the former things, nor consider the things of
old. Behold, God is doing a new thing in my life, and now
it shall spring forth. (Isaiah 43:18–19)

I can do all things through Him who gives me strength.
(Philippians 4:13)

God gives strength to the weary and increases power to the
weak. (Isaiah 40:29)

I am strong in the Lord and in His mighty power. (Ephesians
6:10)

His grace is sufficient for me, and His strength is made perfect
in my weakness. (2 Corinthians 12:9)

God knows the plans He has for me, plans for welfare and
not evil, to give me a future and a hope. (Jeremiah
29:11)

But one thing I do: forgetting what is behind and straining
toward what is ahead, I press toward the goal for the high
calling in Christ Jesus. (Philippians 3:13–14)

This is the confidence that I have in Him, that if I ask
anything according to His will, He hears me. And if I

know that He hears me, whatever I ask, I know that I have
the petitions that I have asked of Him. (1 John 5:14–15)
I will be exceedingly generous, and I will be exceedingly
prosperous. (Proverbs 11:25)

Behind-the-Scenes Habits
That Drive Crazy Success

HABIT #7

Speak up by making positive declarations over your
ideal future self. It's the alone advantage that leads to
transforming your self-image.

It is written: "I believed; therefore I have spoken."
Since we have that same spirit of faith, we also
believe and therefore speak.
—2 CORINTHIANS 4:13

PART 8

Cheer Up!

CHAPTER 22

You Have Something to Be Grateful For

Until you learn to be grateful for the things you have,
you will not receive the things you want.
—JOHN KRALIK

At age fifty-three, an attorney named John Kralik found himself at a low place in life. His small law firm was nearly going under. Among many things, he'd been in a lawsuit, he couldn't pay his staff, and he was under the pressure of a painful second divorce. He had grown apart from his two older children, he was unable to keep up with his bills, he was forty pounds overweight, plus, the only positive thing in his life had been his girlfriend, and she'd just broken up with him. As if this weren't depressing enough, his life dream of becoming a judge seemed utterly hopeless.

During a lonely walk in the hills on New Year's Day, John was struck by the belief that his life might become at least bearable if, instead of focusing on what he didn't have, he could find some way to be grateful for what he did have.

John decided to set the goal of writing 365 thank-you notes in the coming new year (one for every day of the year). One by one, day after day, he began to focus on gratitude. He wrote letters of gratitude to loved ones, coworkers, past business associates and current foes, to college friends and doctors, to store clerks and handymen, neighbors, and anyone, really, absolutely anyone, who had done anything for him.

John's entire life turned around. For example, when John sent a handwritten thank-you card to someone who owed him money, with no ulterior motive other than gratitude, the guy sent him the $4,000 he owed him.

Surprising benefits and blessings began to come John's way. Bottom line: his whole life has been restored and transformed. He's wealthy, he's healthy, he lost the weight, he is happy with his life, he became a bestselling author, and he achieved his lifelong dream of being appointed a judge at a superior court.[1]

. . .

What do successful people do in private so they're rewarded in public? They magnify the good in their life no matter what's going on around them. They voice their appreciation to God. The more gratitude you express, the more abundance you experience!

If you want to start a new chapter in your life, start focusing on the good that is happening. As Jane Fuller says, "a grateful heart is truly a magnet for miracles." Gratitude has been called the secret to life, the key that opens all doors, the cure for creativity, even the antidote for sleepless nights! And the attitude of gratitude comes from God's Word.

Scripture says, "Enter into His gates with thanksgiving *and* a thank offering and into His courts with praise! Be thankful *and* say so to Him, bless *and* affectionately praise His name!" (Psalm 100:4 AMPC). From that verse I picture gratitude as a gate opener. When you start your mornings thanking God for what is happening in your life, it's as if you pushed the gate code and walked right into God's presence.

No matter where you are in life, you have something to be grateful for. As soon as you recognize it and express it, your life will start to improve. Your health, your career, your relationships, your finances, and your opportunities are all affected by your attitude of gratitude. Like attracts like.

Sometimes we just need a little shift in our perspective to realize we truly have an abundance of things to appreciate. If your everyday problems are weighing you down, there are millions of people on earth who would gladly trade places with you right now—problems and all—and feel they had been royally blessed.

Jack Canfield explains,

> The law of attraction says that you will attract into your life whatever you focus on. Whatever you give your energy and attention to will come back to you. So, if you stay focused on the good and positive things in your life, you will automatically attract more good and positive things into your life. If you are focused upon lack and negativity, then that is what will be attracted into your life.[2]

Throughout this book, we've identified the daily habits of some of the most successful people in the world, but can you easily spot the habits of the unsuccessful? You probably can. Did you know that people can identify exactly how successful or unsuccessful you are the moment you open your mouth and *complain*? Ouch! I know, I don't like that either. The truth is, the only thing complaining does is convince other people that you are not in control.

If you're not going to make changes in your finances, to your body, or at your place of employment, then don't complain about them. You chose it, you spent it, you ate it, you settled there. So don't complain about it. I know that is a little harsh. I'm usually more gentle, but I'm only sharing with you what God had to ingrain in me.

It may be quite surprising to recognize how many things you complain about in any given day. The traffic, the weather, how you slept, your hunger, your hair, the red light that took too long, where you had to park, how crowded the restaurant was, if the food was cold, your head hurting, your long list of to-dos, and how tired you are. The list is endless. And we do it without even noticing we're doing it.

Here's the result. When you complain about your life, what you'll get is a lot more to complain about. Why is this? You get what you focus on. It's no different from focusing on red cars. Pretty soon you'll see red cars everywhere. Complaining magnifies the negatives in your life so much that it crowds out the potential for you to see anything positive. "Complaining is also very contagious," said Heather Luszczyk. "It spreads, and it brings others around you down."[3]

Indulge in this slightly and you might as well forget the future. Jim Rohn said to spend five minutes complaining and you will enter a financial desert. Choke on the dust of your own regret!

Consider the story of the Israelites headed to the promised land, the land of abundance. They delayed their arrival by forty years. Why? Because they obsessively complained. They griped about the water, the weather, the food, the leadership, the distance, the climate, the desert, the people. Most surprising? A journey that could have lasted less than two weeks ended up dragging on for more than four decades.

What circumstances are you circling year after year, making very little progress due to your enormous number of complaints? Is it the mountain of weight loss you keep going around, but rather than focus on progress, you magnify the lack of results? Complain and you'll remain.

Could it be the mountain of marital problems? Rather than pinpoint the good in your spouse, you zero in on the bad and magnify it to such a degree that it crowds out any potential for restoration? Complain and you'll remain.

Could it be the mountain of financial problems? Rather than focus on paying off one single debt, you get so overwhelmed at the pile of bills, the lack of savings, the absence of hope for change, and you complain that it will never improve. Complain and you'll remain.

Expressing gratitude is one of the greatest habits to retrain your mind for success. Successful people are grateful people. Think about it this way: Have you ever met an unhappy person who was grateful or a happy person who was ungrateful? Probably not. How do you change a lousy, self-pitying, complaining, discouraged attitude? With appreciation.

. . .

Years ago, when I was faced with the most difficult time in my life, the last thing I wanted to do was express gratitude. *For what?* I thought. *I have nothing to be thankful for! Nothing. My life is falling apart. My marriage is falling apart. I have no peace. I'm miserable!* Those were my dominant thoughts.

As I've shared throughout this book, I came to a place in my life of total desperation. I was in dire need of a turnaround. One day I heard a minister say, "Stop looking at everything you've lost in your life and start looking at everything you have left. And start thanking God for it."

I began to learn that praise, thanksgiving, and a heart of gratitude touch God's heart and literally open the door for Him to start working in my life. I was also learning that voicing my complaints is an open door for the enemy to continue destroying my life.

I remember it like it was yesterday: the first time I tried to start magnifying what I did have and praising God for it. It was late one weekday night, my little girl was upstairs asleep, my husband was living at his mom's house, and sadness, hopelessness, and dread were consuming my mind. I didn't want to lie in bed with my thought life in constant agony.

I walked downstairs to my kitchen with only the light from the hallway on. With tears pouring down my cheeks, I forced myself to lift my hands and say, "Thank You, Father, for—"

I had to pause and think. *What do I have to be thankful for?* I had to dig up something. Surely there was one thing in my life to appreciate. Suddenly it dawned on me.

"Thank you, Father, for my precious little redheaded girl sleeping upstairs. I prayed for a baby after losing one, and then you gave me the very desire of my heart. Lord, I'm so grateful for Kassidi Cherie. Thank You so much for choosing me to be her mother."

I walked in a circle around my island in the kitchen and another thought came to me.

"Thank You, Father, for my best friend, Theresa. She knows everything I'm going through and she still loves me, takes my phone calls, encourages me, and believes in me."

Another lap around the island.

"Thank You, Lord, for my job. I am so grateful I didn't lose my job with all this turmoil going on in my life. And I love my job."

The laps continued and continued.

"Thank You, Jesus, for this house. It's a beautiful house. I'm so grateful I get to live here."

The list went on and on, and here's the kicker. Each time I voiced my appreciation, the sadness felt like it physically lifted off me. The misery would start to fade. And joy, true joy, would be released in my heart. It was a tangible feeling of breathing lighter, experiencing peace, and preparing for a night of good sleep.

I cannot put a price tag on the value of praising, thanking, and appreciating what God has done in your life and what it will produce in your future.

Listen to what God says: "Do not fret *or* have any anxiety about anything, but in every circumstance *and* in everything, by prayer and petition (definite requests), *with thanksgiving*, continue to make your wants known to God" (Philippians 4:6 AMPC).

Those two little words, *with thanksgiving*, have more impact than you can imagine.

CHAPTER 23

5 Reasons Successful People Keep a Gratitude Journal

The struggle ends when gratitude begins.
—NEALE DONALD WALSCH

n 1943 S. I. Kisher published a short story about a soldier during World War II. The soldier was a young guy in Florida who visited the local library one day. He picked up a book and noticed little notes in the margin (handwritten and very heartfelt). He looked in the front of the book and noticed the name of the previous owner and her address. This was way before Google. Her name was Holly and she lived in New York City.

The soldier was so intrigued that he sent Holly a letter, introducing himself, and explaining that he was headed to Europe to serve his country in the war. But would she mind staying in touch so they could compare notes about the book that she'd annotated?

Holly wrote back. The young man had a delightful surprise when he was handed the first of her letters to him while he was stationed overseas. Thus began more than a year of getting to know each other through the mail until a friendship became love. Quite unexpectedly this couple was falling in love with each other through words even though they'd never met or even exchanged photos. (There was no Instagram either.)

After a while the soldier requested a picture of his lovely pen pal, but Holly declined. (Are you thinking what I'm thinking? The first "catfish" took place! Ha!) Finally, after many months of war and journeying home, the soldier found out that his route would take him through New York City. Holly and he could meet in person for the first time.

He asked her to dinner, and she told him, "I'll be waiting for you when you get off the ship. You'll know it's me by the pink flower in my hair." The soldier was happy and nervous at the same time. The moment arrived and he disembarked from his ship onto American soil just as an exquisite young woman approached. Her beauty stunned him, and he was so distracted in admiring her that it took him a moment to realize the most important detail. This gorgeous lady didn't have a flower in her hair.

In a breath she strode away through the crowd, and the soldier tried to refocus his attention on finding Holly. Another woman began approaching him—a bit older and much less attractive, her face showing the beginning of wrinkles. A pink rose was tucked in her graying hair.

Purposing to hide his disappointment, the soldier squared his shoulders, saluted her, and greeted her with a warm smile as he remembered the woman he'd grown to love through letters. "Hello, ma'am, you must be Holly. I'm so glad to finally meet you. May I take you to dinner?"

The woman smiled back and said, "Son, I'm not sure what's going on here, but the young lady who just passed you asked me to wear this pink flower, and then she said that if you invited me to dinner, to tell you she'll be waiting for you in the restaurant across the street."[1]

. . .

It was a test! Will you do the right thing when it's hard, when you don't understand it—or feel especially grateful for it? Don't give up hope. God will not only give you the desires of your heart but even more when you do what's right even when it's hard.

Will you praise God with tears pouring down your face because your marriage is ripping your heart out? Will you be grateful when the promotion is given to one of your coworkers? Will you still have a heart of appreciation when you've been practicing these success habits and it appears nothing is changing?

Just like in my personal story, you must decide to magnify the good that is happening in your life and stop focusing on all that's not right. Change your perspective and you'll change your outcome.

> Change your perspective and you'll change your outcome.

When I opened my first office in 2014, I felt impressed to begin my weekly staff meetings with gratitude. I initiated the first meeting by giving out little sticky notepads around the table to my team. I said, "Write down a few things you're grateful for since we moved here." They began writing. One by one we moved around the table reading from our Post-it Notes, voicing our gratitude for all God had done. You can't help but be encouraged by the atmosphere produced by this simple procedure. Some team members remembered things others forgot. Others recognized little things that not everyone had thought of. I told everyone to share as big or as small as they wanted. Nothing was insignificant. They began sharing things such as this:

"All the new people we met in Boston last week at the conference."
"Our YouTube subscribers have already doubled in a couple of months!"
"Our new book release."
"That I get to work with the greatest team members here!"
"We received the largest donation we've ever received."

"The testimony of a fourteen-year-old girl who stopped cutting
   herself after hearing our messages."
"The forty people we prayed with at the altar last Wednesday
   night."
"The invitation this week to speak at a new success conference."
"The environment we get to work in."

The gratitude was endless. Here's the key: since that day we haven't stopped doing this, but we also have never lacked for something to be grateful for! Week after week we open each team meeting with thankfulness. Not one time have we been speechless. Consistently, we are overwhelmed at how much we have to be grateful for just since the previous Wednesday's meeting! And now it's turned into placing Post-its on a gigantic "gratitude wall." It's a constant reminder of our appreciation to God.

When you begin expressing gratitude, especially when your circumstances are less than pleasant, you're likely to try your best to "look on the bright side" and say things such as:

"I'm grateful that I at least have a roof over my head."
"I'm grateful that I at least have food to eat."
"I'm grateful that I at least have a job."
"I'm grateful that I at least have a car."

All of these "at least" expressions are an attempt to build some sort of positive momentum, but deep down, you're not genuinely that thrilled about it. When you get a deep revelation of how powerful your expressions of praise, thanksgiving, and gratitude are, your circumstances become irrelevant because you know they're about to change in your favor.

. . .

The University of Massachusetts Dartmouth did an in-depth study on the effects of gratitude and discovered just how much it can contribute to your rate of success. People who show more gratitude are reported to have higher levels of alertness, enthusiasm, determination, attentiveness, and energy, and they also get better sleep.[2]

Success coaches advise that gratitude is one of the greatest attributes of successful people. Much research has been done on why employees leave a job. Here are some commonly cited stats that are ascribed to Jack Canfield, and similar numbers are frequently cited on this topic:

46 percent said they leave a job because they feel unappreciated,

61 percent said it's because their bosses don't place enough importance on them as people, and

88 percent said they leave because they don't receive acknowledgment for the work they do.

Appreciation is important. Acknowledging appreciation is very important to your coworkers, your family, your friends, and especially to God. In fact, BCG's survey of 200,000 employees found that appreciation is "the most important single job element."[3]

One of the best ways to cultivate appreciation is by keeping a gratitude journal. This has benefits that impact nearly every area of your life.

- Television host Steve Harvey said, "Gratitude is a powerful process. The only way to move to the next level is you must show gratitude for where you are. If you show gratitude, it gets you to where you want to be quicker."
- Actress Camila Mendes admits that writing gratitude in her journal "helped relieve the stress and anxiety by shifting the focus of her life to center around the good things in everyday life instead of obsessively grieving over the bad things that come with fame."[4]

- Actor Will Arnett said, "I write down ten things I'm grateful for every day."[5]
- Actor Chris Pratt said, "Usually before I eat a meal I'll list the things for which I'm grateful."[6]
- Country singer Brett Eldredge keeps a gratitude journal, primarily to remember things that have happened.[7]

The benefits of journaling your gratitude to retrain your mind for success are endless. Following are my top five.

1. Less Stress

It's been proven that focusing on feelings of appreciation naturally counters stress. When you focus on the good things in life rather than the pressures, your stress levels naturally lower. One study found that after twenty-one days of journaling your gratitude, you retrain your brain to start automatically looking for the positives. After forty-two days, levels of depression and anxiety decrease and levels of happiness increase.[8]

2. Greater Self-Esteem

Journaling gratitude about your personal life helps you appreciate what God is doing for you, rather than comparing your life with what's happening around you. You're less likely to envy others when you magnify your thankfulness to God.

3. Better Sleep

Research shows that before you turn in for the night, focusing your mind on a few things you are grateful for will lead to a much better night's sleep. By thinking of the uplifting things that happened during your day or reminding yourself of something you are thankful for, you clear your mind of anxiety and restlessness, promoting peaceful sleep.[9]

4. Increased Optimism

This is an obvious byproduct of gratitude. As you shift your focus from complaining to gratitude, you naturally become more optimistic. Instead of scanning the world looking for negativity, you'll be magnifying all the amazing things in life. And you'll be a much more pleasant person to be around.

5. Mood Boost

Writing what you're grateful for makes your memories feel more real and concrete. As you reflect on previous entries, you can't help but feel a boost in your mood as you realize entry after entry is proof that good things are happening in your life. The more grateful you are, the more you'll have to journal about.

. . .

We sure seem to love challenges. I filmed several YouTube videos offering thirty-day challenges on a variety of topics such as "Do countertop push-ups to sculpt your arms," "Floss your teeth before bed," "Drink apple cider vinegar when you wake up," "Make your bed," and "Keep a food journal."

People responded to those videos more than any other videos all year. I couldn't believe it. And you might wonder, *Why thirty days?* and *Why even do these challenges?*

Well, I found out that within thirty days you can make a massive

179

difference to your life without spending tons of money or reinventing your whole self. You can develop new habits that will improve your health, your productivity, and your finances, and also seriously set you up for success.

It's just a month-long period where you implement small, simple actions that can either help you start new habits or help you stop some old ones. And challenging yourself is so good for you. Plus it builds your confidence, your self-esteem, and your momentum to go after bigger goals in life. Thirty days is a perfect amount of time to really push yourself without feeling overwhelmed. So are you up for a good challenge?

The Gratitude Challenge

Take the Twenty-Four-Hour Test

I want you to embark on a full day of no complaining whatsoever for twenty-four hours. I'll be honest, it's a bit harder than you think. Do not complain that you woke up late, don't complain about the weather, the traffic, the bad hair day, the nuisance of having to get gas, the frequent red lights, the coworkers popping into your office, the baby crying all night, the hassle of cooking, the deadline that's coming up, the soccer game you must attend—your life in general. No complaints for twenty-four hours.

David Horsager, bestselling author of *The Trust Edge*, said, "I remember a mentor of mine twenty years ago said, 'David . . . I want you to try not complaining one time about anything for ninety days. . . . It changed the trajectory of my life.'"[10] His clients have included Wells Fargo, Goodyear, the Department of Homeland Security, and the New York Yankees! It all began with his making a commitment to stop complaining.

Philippians 2:14 says, "Do *all things* without grumbling and fault-finding and complaining" (AMPC). That's a clear command.

Write Down Things You're Grateful For

Plan to do this during your prayer/meditation routine or before you go to bed each night. Make sure you do it at the same time each day so it can become a habit.

Write whatever comes up in your heart. It doesn't have to be big, major things, such as the raise, the new car, or the exotic vacation. It can be as simple as the day off at home, the sun shining, the cupcake your friend brought you, or the new book you just purchased. It doesn't have to be huge, enormous breakthrough occurrences—those rarely happen on a daily basis.

Thank the Lord for the food in your pantry, your closet full of clothing, and the bed you slept in. When you open the refrigerator door and "can't find anything to eat," thank the Lord for the pleasure of getting to eat three meals a day. Thank the Lord for your job and think about those who are unemployed month after month. Thank the Lord for your health as you think about those waking up again in a hospital bed. Thank the Lord for your computer or your phone and its ability to connect you with friends and family all over the world.

Journal Your Gratitude for Thirty Days

I'm telling you from experience and from the testimonies of thousands, when you do this your life will be on a path to success. God will open doors in your life that you never dreamed possible. Why? Because you're acknowledging every single thing He does and you're giving no attention to the distractions complaining brings.

You will be utterly amazed at how a simple shift in your attitude from complaining to expressing gratitude can bring such fulfillment, absolute relief from stress and anxiety, an appearance of blessings, an atmosphere of peace, a sense of the presence of God, strength in your body, and realization of your dreams.

CHAPTER 24

Get God's Attention

Say thank you in advance for what's already
yours. That's how I live my life. That's one of
the reasons I am where I am today.
—DENZEL WASHINGTON

Would you have ever believed that raspy rocker Rod Stewart was employed as a gravedigger in a London cemetery before he became an international singing sensation? Or that actor Hugh Jackman worked as a gym teacher who moonlighted as a party clown for fifty dollars a gig? Or what about Dr. McDreamy from *Grey's Anatomy*, actor Patrick Dempsey, who was a professional juggler and performed with Cirque du Soleil?[1]

Just as their dreams of singing and acting may have seemed utterly impossible, your dreams probably seem equally as unachievable. You don't know how God can accomplish them. You don't know the right people. You don't have the finances. You don't have any connections or spectacular opportunities being handed your way. All you know is that God told you to dream. Now all He's asking you to do is believe.

There's a story in the Bible of two men who were blind and approached Jesus, asking if He would give them their sight. Instead of instantly healing the men, Jesus put the responsibility back on them by asking one pivotal question: "Do you believe that I am able to do this?" (Matthew 9:28). The key to their breakthrough was in their response. Without hesitation the men proclaimed, "Why, yes, Master!" (MSG). Jesus then touched their eyes and gave the solution to any of us desiring an impossible dream: "Become what you believe" (verse 29 MSG).

Just as those men began to see outwardly, you need to see your dream inwardly as if it's already happened. You need to have bold faith in God's ability to do what seems impossible. Imagine Jesus standing before you today asking, "Do you really think I can give you that business, that career, that ministry, that financial breakthrough, that relationship goal?" And without hesitation, you boldly say, "Yes, Lord."

You don't have to know how He is going to bring your dreams about; you only need to trust that He will.

The Highest Expression of Your Faith

Now, take it a step further and start thanking God in advance for what He is *about to do* in your life.

This is the highest expression of your faith. Did you read that? Read it again.

When you thank God *before* your breakthrough, you have just demonstrated the highest expression of your faith. It shows just how much you trust Him. It communicates that you really believe He loves you. You're so convinced, you're going to thank Him in advance.

If you really think about it, you already demonstrate that extreme faith in people whom you trust who make promises to you. For example, I remember years ago when I began my ICING Women's Event, a friend called my office and spoke with my assistant, Donna. He expressed that he was so touched by our outreach to young women, rescuing them from human trafficking and giving them tools to help place them on a path to success, that he wanted to completely underwrite the budget of our next ICING conference.

Immediately Donna called me as I was on my way back to the office to share this extraordinary news. I almost had to pull over on the side of the road, as I was in complete shock. "What? He's going to pay for the whole event?"

"Yes," Donna said. "He asked me for the budget, I told him, and he's sending a check."

After I shouted "Thank You, Jesus!" I asked Donna to give me his number so I could personally thank him. Then I asked her to send him a Bundt cake with a note that read: "You're nothing Bundt the best. Thank you for helping us spread ICING" (I love puns).

As soon as we hung up, I called my friend and profusely thanked him for being so incredibly generous, and I prayed that God would multiply his significant seed into our ministry and bless him just as extravagantly.

Now, think about it. My response to my friend doesn't seem so fanatical, does it? Don't you normally thank people who do nice things for you? But here's my point: I thanked my friend, and I even sent him a gift of gratitude *before* I ever saw the check. Why? I had faith in his word. I trust him. I know him. I thoroughly believed he would do what he said he would do, so I went ahead and told him how much I appreciated it.

Well, God is not a man that He should lie. He already said this:

- "No good thing will He withhold from those who walk uprightly." (Psalm 84:11 NKJV)
- "If you delight yourself in Him, He will give you the desires of your heart." (Psalm 37:4, author paraphrase)
- "Therefore I tell you, whatever you ask for in prayer, believe that you have received it, and it will be yours." (Mark 11:24)

Go ahead and thank Him for what you believe He is about to do in your life. Each morning as I go through my habits, this one is where I simply look at my vision board and I speak my dreams out loud, thanking the Lord ahead of time for what He is about to do in my life. Many successful people write their goals down every single day as part of their rituals. I, however, only do this in the month of January, when I write them down every day for thirty days. For the remainder of the year I give life to my dreams by speaking to them and expressing gratitude to God for what He is about to do in my life. Do whatever you feel makes your dreams come alive, and stay alive as you're waiting for them to manifest.

Consider the example of Paul and Silas when they had been arrested (Acts 16:16–40). They were beaten, bruised, battered, and in pain. They were imprisoned with no visible hope of ever getting out. But the Bible records that in the midnight hour, which signifies the darkest hour, they began to lift their voices to heaven in praise and adoration of their God.

Their praise wasn't silent either. They didn't whisper *thanks*. No, Scripture reveals their voices were so loud that the other prisoners could hear them. And what happened next is solid proof of the impact your gratitude has on Almighty God.

An earthquake was sent from heaven that shook the entire prison. The earth began to crumble, the walls began to shake, the steel chains fell off their feet, and the prison doors opened up!

This supernatural event would never have happened had Paul and Silas not praised and thanked God before the victory. Your life will never change until you begin vocalizing what you believe God intends to do for you.

Praising God in your midnight hour, behind closed doors when it seems like the craziest thing to do, will open doors in your life that you never dreamed possible!

The Depth of Your Praise

Vital Key: You must feel it!

This truth is so vital that I had to put it front and center to make you really see it. You absolutely must feel as if you already have what you are asking God for. That means fists clenched, wide-smiled, squealing with exhilaration because you know that you know that you know it's done! Your dreams are en route to your house! When you praise God with that much enthusiasm, it gets His attention. He sees your faith! And it's impossible to please God without faith.

Imagine going to the movie theater to see an exciting drama or adventure film. You arrive ten minutes before the earlier showing has ended. Instead of waiting in the lobby, you go inside the theater and watch the last ten minutes of the film. You see how the entire plot unfolds and how everything turns out. When the next showing starts, you go back in and sit through the entire movie, but instead of being on the edge of your seat—nervous, concerned, anxious—you watch the details of the clothing, the camera angles, the background. You're trying to think of other movies you've seen the actor in. You're not nervous at all. You're calm, relaxed, and taking time to enjoy the acting. Why? You already know how it all ends!

This is exactly how you need to act about your future. If you really trust that God is in control and that He works all things together for your good (Romans 8:28 paraphrase), then start praising Him ahead of time!

Behind-the-Scenes Habits
That Drive Crazy Success

HABIT #8

Cheer up by journaling your gratitude, praising God for what He is doing and what He is about to do in your life. It's the alone advantage that leads to God opening doors that you never dreamed possible.

Enter into His gates with thanksgiving *and* a thank offering and into His courts with praise! Be thankful *and* say so to Him, bless *and* affectionately praise His name!
—PSALM 100:4 AMPC

PART 9

Step Up!

CHAPTER 25

Give God What You've Got

The separation is in the preparation.
—ED MYLETT

There's an island in the Bahamas that used to be called Hog Island because of the pigs that roamed it. Today Hog Island is known as Paradise Island, home to the extravagant Atlantis resort. How do you move from hogs to hotels? When others saw a pigpen, someone else saw a way to "bring home the bacon." They saw potential. It's not what you have, it's how you develop what you have.

God sees potential in you. You need to realize it and develop it. I heard this phrase come up in my spirit in prayer one morning, and I wrote it in my journal: "Give Me what you've got, and I'll turn it into a lot." I continued to hear this in my heart from the Lord: "When you give Me what appears small, I take what you have and give you My all."

God was saying that He can do so much with so little. He has a way of choosing the least likely people to do some of the most amazing things. Look at this list of what most would consider little potential.

Cripple [a man] and you have Sir Walter Scott.
Lock him in prison and you have John Bunyan.
Bury him in the snows of Valley Forge and you have George Washington.

Raise him in poverty and you have Abraham Lincoln.

Strike him down with infantile paralysis and he becomes Franklin Delano Roosevelt.

Burn him so severely that doctors say he will never walk again, and you have Glen Cunningham, who set the world's record in 1934 for the outdoor mile.

Deafen him and you'll have Ludwig van Beethoven.

Call him a slow learner and write him off as uneducable and you have Albert Einstein.[1]

And I would like to add one more to the list of least-likely people: Violate her, abuse her, fill her with crippling insecurities until she sinks into a miserable rut, and you have bestselling author and motivational speaker Terri Savelle Foy.

. . .

What will your sentence say? What are you willing to give to God so He can mold it, refine it, and turn your story into a masterpiece to inspire someone else?

I was reading a sermon by Kenneth Morris in which he mentions what happens to a lobster when it leaves its shell. Of course, it needs its shell for protection, but as it grows, the old shell must be left behind. If the lobster doesn't abandon it, the old shell will trap it until it cannot get out and is stuck inside until it dies.

Morris says, "The tricky part for the lobster is that brief period of time between when the old shell is discarded and the new one is formed. During that terribly vulnerable period, the transition must be scary for the lobster" because the ocean is tossing it all over the place and fish are ready to eat it alive.[2]

To change, to grow, to seize the dreams God has for you, you must abandon your shell, your old life, your old patterns and ways of doing things. Don't miss your time because you stayed stuck in the shell of your past. God is getting you ready to start a new chapter. Start with acknowledging that deeper longing within you. And start perfecting your skills in private.

I want to push you to *step up* and prepare now. Study now. Design now. Write your resume now. Take photographs now. Write the music now. Practice the song now. Rehearse now. Take the classes now. Why? Prepare in private so you can seize the opportunities to use your talents in public.

Years ago a certain woman worked as a church secretary and also served on the church's music team. Then she took the worship music world by storm when she offered her song "Shout to the Lord" for the music team's new recording. Darlene Zschech prepared behind the scenes and now her music has sold millions of albums worldwide.

What if Darlene

- had convinced herself she wasn't *that good* of a songwriter?
- had talked herself out of finishing the song because she assumed no one would ever hear it?
- had allowed others to discourage her from singing and writing music because that wasn't in her job description?
- had allowed the busyness of day-to-day work to stop her from investing time in pursuing her real passion of singing and writing music?

Prepare now. Don't wait another year to pursue what you are most passionate about. Be ready when God brings an opportunity your way.

All those hours you are spending reading books in your field of interest, attending classes after school or work, researching online, investing money in learning more, practicing

> Don't wait another year to pursue what you are most passionate about.

day after day, reading *this* book, keeping your commitment to wake up early—you are not wasting time. You are preparing for opportunities. Preparation time is never wasted time.

' ' '

When he was in high school, basketball great Larry Bird would shoot five hundred free throws every morning before his first class.[3] Actor Jim Carrey would sit in front of a mirror contorting his face for hours and perfecting his skills.[4] Basketball legend Michael Jordan practiced his jump shot hundreds of times per day during the offseason.[5] Winston Churchill, one of the twentieth century's greatest orators, practiced his speeches compulsively.[6]

Vladimir Horowitz, one of the greatest pianists of all time, reportedly said, "If I don't practice for a day, I know it. If I don't practice for two days, my wife knows it. If I don't practice for three days, the world knows it."[7]

The ones who make it look effortless are the ones who practice the most when nobody is looking. If you want to achieve the dreams God has put in your heart, get focused behind the scenes.

I heard a fun, albeit apocryphal, story about the famous artist Picasso. He ran into a lady at a market one day and she said, "Picasso, can you draw a portrait for me?"

"Of course," said Picasso.

Within thirty seconds he sketched a portrait that looked identical to the lady in front of him.

He reached out his hand and said, "That will be thirty thousand dollars."

"Picasso!" she shouted. "How can you charge me thirty thousand dollars when it only took you thirty seconds to draw it?"

To which Picasso replied, "Ma'am, it took me thirty years to be able to do that in thirty seconds."

The further you go in life, the more preparation it will require. And preparation takes place *behind the scenes* with nobody watching. Everything good in my life today is a result of what I gained in privacy yesterday.

You have skills that can lead to an abundant life. Every day you spend learning, growing, and sharpening your skills, you're getting prepared. And when God is looking for somebody to promote, you'll be ready.

It's time to step up and start preparing behind the scenes.

CHAPTER 26

5 Things Successful People Quit

Expecting the world to treat you fairly just because
you're a good person is a little like expecting the bull
not to charge you because you're a vegetarian.
—DENNIS WHOLEY

enzel Washington had a difficult time finding his career path. When he enrolled in college, he decided to major in premed, then he changed to political science, and then to prelaw. He discovered that he wasn't doctor material or lawyer material, so he started studying journalism. However, with no academic focus, his grades declined. The university recommended he take some time off.

Although Denzel worked at many different places to make ends meet—including a factory and a post office—he slowly fell in love with acting. Even though he'd finally discovered his true passion, it wasn't an easy road. He had many failures, but he describes them as "falling forward"—every failure simply one step closer to success. Everyone fails. We must accept that. It's part of the journey to success. It's part of our story.

Eventually, every step of failure led Denzel to a path of massive success. He's won several Oscars and is one of the most respected actors in Hollywood. While giving a commencement address, Denzel said,

When you go through life feeling scared and insecure, remember to not only take risks, but to be open to life; to accept new views, and to be open to new opinions. While it may be frightening, it will also be rewarding. Because the chances you take . . . the people you meet . . . the people you love . . . the Faith that you have—that's what's going to define your life. Never be discouraged. Never hold back. Give everything you've got. Remember this: fall forward.[1]

It can be frustrating when you're waiting on a dream to manifest, but don't start questioning God or trying to figure out how to help Him. Nothing good grows overnight. It's a process. Put your complete trust in His timing, and it will eliminate aggravation and worry. God will cause your dream to manifest right on time.

. . .

In his book *Become a Better You*, Joel Osteen explains what it's like to stay focused.

I talked to a famous tightrope walker, who comes from a family of seven generations of circus entertainers. I asked him, "What is the key to walking on the tightrope? You make it look so easy."

He said, "Joel, the secret is to keep your eyes fixed on where you are going. You never look down. Where your head goes, that's where your body is going too. If you look down, there's a good chance you will fall. So, you always have to look to where you want to be."

It's the same principle in life. Some people are always looking back, focused on their hurts and pains. Other people are looking down, living in self-pity, and complaining that life is not fair. The key to rising higher is to keep looking to where you want to go. Dream big dreams! Don't focus on where you are today; keep a positive vision and see yourself accomplishing your goals and fulfilling your destiny.[2]

Part of staying focused is knowing what to do, and another part is knowing what to quit. Here are five things that successful people quit as they are falling forward and focusing on the future.

1. Making Excuses

Excuses are what we give ourselves when we don't want to admit that we are where we are because of us, our choices. They're subtle reasons you create to justify why you can't succeed. The truth is we can always find grounds not to pursue our goals. After all, our reasons are *reasonable*.

There's a quote attributed to Benjamin Franklin that says, "He that is good for making excuses is seldom good for anything else." (Franklin also chose the motto on the American dollar bill—*Annuit cœptis*—which basically means that God favors bold enterprises.[3])

They say that if you really want something, you will find a way. If you don't, you'll find an excuse. Zig Ziglar said that people who are prone to making excuses "say things like, 'I'd go back to college and get my degree, but it would take six years and by then I'd be thirty-eight.' (I wonder how old they will be in six years if they don't go back and get their degree?)"[4] Good point.

I don't have the education. *Start reading.*
Nobody believes in me. *Believe in yourself.*
It's never been done before. *Be the first to do it.*
I'm too busy. *Schedule time.*
I've made too many mistakes. *Forgive yourself and move on.*
It's too late. *Start focusing on the time you have left and use it wisely.*
This just isn't the right time. *And it never will be if you keep making excuses.*

It's so easy to make them. You must ask yourself, "How badly do I want progress in my life?" When you truly desire a goal or a dream, you will eliminate any excuse and rise to the occasion to achieve it. Taking responsibility for where you are in life at this very moment is the foundation for success. Living an excuse-free life starts you on the pathway to succeed.

Embrace the journey, challenge yourself, learn new things, be vulnerable, stick your neck out, stop playing it safe, and prove to yourself that you have what it takes to succeed in life.

2. Doubting

Software engineer Brian Acton wanted to be on the cutting edge of technology. He had twelve years of experience at Yahoo and was a software mastermind, but his dream job was to work for Facebook or Twitter. Neither of the social media giants would hire him. After Twitter rejected him, Brian tweeted: Got denied by Twitter HQ. That's ok. Would have been a long commute.

After being rejected by Facebook, he responded with a Facebook post: Facebook turned me down. It was a great opportunity to connect with some fantastic people. Looking forward to life's next adventure.

Although he was rejected by his two dream companies, Brian stuck with his desire to be involved with the latest technology. He decided to team up with a former coworker at Yahoo and began creating his own app. Five years later he sold that app to Facebook (of all companies) for a reported $19 billion! Brian Acton is the cocreator of WhatsApp.[5]

No matter how many setbacks you have, rejections you encounter, or disappointments you experience, you must believe in yourself. Your dreams are part of the overall assignment God has placed on your life.

We all have doubts, insecurities, fears. I'm the one who needed fifty-seven confirmations before I resigned as CEO to start my own organization! But if you journal your time with the Lord and write down key insights you're learning, you'll clearly see where God is leading you and let it eliminate your doubts of stepping out.

3. Expecting the Worst

You tend to get exactly what you expect in life. In *See You at the Top*, Zig Ziglar tells a true story about Teresa Jones of Wilmington, Delaware:

> [She] had a serious kidney infection. An operation was scheduled to remove one of the kidneys. After they put her to sleep, they ran the final test and discovered that the operation was not necessary. They didn't remove the kidney, but when she awoke the first thing she said was, "Oh, my back. Oh, I hurt. Oh, I feel so bad. Oh, it hurts." When Teresa was told they did not perform the operation, she was slightly embarrassed. Obviously, she went to sleep expecting to wake up hurting, and that is exactly what she did.[6]

Successful people quit expecting the worst. They program their mind for greatness through the messages they hear and the words they speak.

4. Living in Fear

"The thing which I greatly feared is come upon me" (Job 3:25 KJV). Don't feed your fears by entertaining them in your mind. Feed your faith by renewing your mind with God's Word, where He reminds us over and over, "Fear not; there is nothing to fear" (Psalm 23:4 and Isaiah 41:10).

5. Expecting Life to Be Easy

You've heard the quote that "Success is 1 percent inspiration and 99 percent perspiration." Jack Canfield was rejected 144 times before he found a publisher for his book *Chicken Soup for the Soul*.[7] Dr. Seuss was rejected by twenty-seven publishers before he started his classic children's series.[8] Walt Disney was rejected by bankers three hundred times because they thought the idea of Mickey Mouse was absurd.[9] You're not an isolated case. Every successful person embraces the struggle.

"Let us not be weary in well doing: for in due season we shall reap, if we faint not" (Galatians 6:9 KJV).

Keith Craft wrote this incredible poem that sums up the mindset of a winner.

Choose Your Hard

Being your best is hard—Being your normal is hard
Making wise decisions is hard—Making bad
    decisions is hard
Being in shape is hard—Being out of shape is hard
Losing weight is hard—Being fat is hard
Working out is hard—Being weak is hard
Being disciplined is hard—Being lazy is hard
Getting out of your comfort zone is hard—Staying
    in your comfort zone is hard
Starting a business is hard—Working for someone
    else is hard

Making a lot of money is hard—Making a little
    bit of money is hard
Being rich is hard—Being poor is hard
Having great relationships is hard—Having bad
    relationships is hard
Fighting for your marriage is hard—Divorce is hard
Having a lot of things is hard—Having nothing is hard
Living on purpose is hard—Living off purpose is hard
Doing life God's way is hard—Doing life your
    own way is hard
Everything is hard! Choose your *hard.*[10]

KEITH CRAFT

CHAPTER 27

Get Ready!

One word helps you do something about one
thing instead of nothing about everything.
—MIKE ASHCRAFT

On Thanksgiving Day 2013 Shonda Rimes, the creator of shows such as *Scandal, Grey's Anatomy,* and *How to Get Away with Murder,* was preparing the family meal with her sister, Delores, when suddenly Delores said six words that changed her life forever: "You never say yes to anything." That statement shook Rimes up and compelled her to choose one three-letter word for an entire year: *yes!*

Why? Because she realized she was saying no to everything! She said no to amazing invitations to be a guest on famous talk shows. She said no to attending awards shows and presenting awards. She declined being around influential people outside of work. She always said no! Why? Because of anxiety, fear, self-doubt, and nervousness.

Rimes decided to start saying yes to nearly everything that pushed her out of her comfort zone, and it opened up a whole new world to her. She's given TED talks about it. She wrote a bestselling book about it. She even became a *New York Times* bestselling author all because she focused on saying one powerful, three-letter word: yes![1]

What could you accomplish in your life if you started saying yes to everything God has put on your heart to do?

Another journal entry during my prayer time that changed my life was this: "When I know you're ready, get ready." Unsure as to what that truly meant, I decided to take it literally and start preparing for the dreams in my heart.

One of them was to write a book. I did exactly what I've been sharing. I wrote the vision. I even went to the bookstore and posed in front of the shelves, acting like I was a published author, and pinned that picture on my vision board. But then I went a step further by taking action.

> We beg you, please don't squander one bit of this marvelous life God has given us.
> —2 CORINTHIANS 6:1 MSG

I blocked time in my daily schedule to start writing. Keep in mind that nobody was knocking on my door asking me to sign a contract. Nobody really cared what I had to say. I didn't have a successful YouTube channel yet. There was no demand to read what I was putting on paper. I was simply obeying what I heard in those quiet times with the Lord. *Get ready.*

I blocked time to write my book every Tuesday and Saturday morning for a couple of months. I cannot count how often discouraging thoughts tried to control my mind, telling me I was wasting my time, nobody would ever read my book, I had nothing good to say, who cares about my foolish dreams, I should be with my family hanging out.

I had to aggressively combat those debilitating thoughts by speaking my positive declarations every morning—not once per month but every single sunrise. I made the affirmations very personal and specific by adding, "I am signing with a publisher before my fortieth birthday."

Months went by and I stuck to my routine, preparing behind the scenes. I finished the manuscript and it sat for months on a little flash drive in my desk. But remember what the Lord spoke to my heart in prayer? *"When I know you're ready, get ready."*

On September 18 I received the contract to publish my book.

My birthday is September 30. I was ready when opportunity came and I seized it! I signed a book deal twelve days before my fortieth birthday.

What did John Wooden say? "When opportunity comes, it's too late to prepare." What are you doing to prepare for what you believe God has called you to do? What's on your calendar for today? Every single day is another opportunity to take action. What does that mean to you personally?

Write another chapter.
Get your resume typed.
Join the gym.
Get your passport.
Save one hundred dollars from this week's paycheck.
Call the university.
Register online.
Ask for a scholarship.
Test drive the car.
Research the business.
Enroll in the class.
Start the lessons.
Call a mentor.
Schedule a meeting.
Plan a trip.

Back when Sylvester Stallone was a struggling actor just scraping by, his life was changed in one moment of decision as he watched a boxing match between Chuck Wepner and world heavyweight champion Muhammad Ali on March 25, 1975.

In the ninth round, underdog Wepner did what no one thought he could do—he knocked the champion to the ground. Fans worldwide were shocked! Although Ali did retain his title, this relatively unknown fighter, Wepner, went an unexpected fifteen rounds with the champ and was only seconds away from winning.

Stallone took immediate action with an idea. He grabbed a pencil and a notepad and began writing the screenplay for what would become the three-time Oscar-winning film *Rocky*.

What if Stallone had thought, "I'll start writing tomorrow." What if tomorrow he wasn't as inspired? What if tomorrow turned into next week and then next month, and then it never resulted in any action? Stallone had a do-it-now mentality and finished the first draft of his screenplay in only three days![2]

W. Clement Stone, who built an insurance empire worth millions of dollars, made his employees repeat "Do it now!" at the start of each workday. He was convinced that this chant would reprogram their thinking and stop delays in their tracks. And he was right.[3]

Procrastination is your best guaranteed route to a life of missed opportunities. When you get inspired to act, if you don't do something within twenty-four hours, chances are that you never will. *Do it now.* Whatever you want to do, do it now! There are only so many tomorrows.

Behind-the-Scenes Habits
That Drive Crazy Success

HABIT #9

Step up and start preparing, getting ready and developing your skills behind the scenes. It's the alone advantage that leads to unprecedented opportunities.

So let's not get tired of doing what is good. At just the right time we will reap a harvest of blessing if we don't give up.
—GALATIANS 6:9 NLT

PART 10

Get Up!

CHAPTER 28

Have You Had Enough?

That which you do not hate you'll eventually tolerate.

—MALCOLM X

Not too long ago, my husband, Rodney, and I watched Tina Turner's life story in the movie *What's Love Got to Do with It?* She was married to Ike Turner, who discovered her and gave her a start in music. But little by little he became very abusive. Slapping her, punching her, even putting her in the hospital. Over and over, year after year, she put up with him. I was sitting there watching this, thinking, *You're "Proud Mary keep on burnin" Tina Turner! Leave him!* But here's what I've discovered: Only you can decide when you've had enough. Only you can determine when enough is enough. Only you can get fed up!

One day, Tina made that decision. She and Ike were in Dallas, Texas, on their way to stay at the Statler Hotel. In the back seat of the limousine, her husband beat her up for the last time. I don't know what it was about that moment in comparison to all the other times he'd abused her, but she'd had enough. While he was asleep on the sofa in the hotel room, she finally made up her mind: *I've had enough!*

With nothing but the clothes on her back and thirty-seven cents in her purse, she ran down the interstate and found a little motel not too far away. She told the manager who she was and promised to pay him back if he would just let her stay there for one night. He had compassion and gave her a complimentary room, and she never looked back. Once Tina decided she had had enough, her career began to soar again. She broke new records and is forever documented in the Rock & Roll Hall of Fame.[1]

. . .

Have you had enough yet? When do you draw the line in your life and say, "I've had enough!"?

> "I've had enough being in debt, living paycheck to paycheck, and barely making it."
> "I've had enough being put down and verbally abused!"
> "I've had enough being out of shape and feeling insecure about myself."
> "I've had enough sitting on the sidelines of life knowing God has more for me."
> "I've had enough living like this!"

It's one thing to hear about the advantage of spending time alone, the importance of purchasing a $7.99 journal and starting these new success habits in private. But are you ready for this discipline yet?

Here's a key: nothing changes if nothing changes. You and only you must decide when you've had enough.

The Bible says, "The devil roams around like a lion roaring [in fierce hunger], seeking someone to seize upon *and* devour" (1 Peter 5:8 AMPC). He's looking to devour you whether it's through laziness, passivity, insecurity, or fear of stepping out—he doesn't care. If you never get fed up, he's fueled up. He knows you'll never reach your full potential until you've had enough of being where you are!

When my life hit that all-time low in 2002, I looked into my future and realized that unless I made a radical decision to change, it wasn't going to be a season of regret but a lifetime of regret. And

I reached the decision of *enough*! I started doing things behind the scenes with nobody around, and it took me from being a woman on the verge of divorce to a wife celebrating thirty-plus years of marriage, from someone with no dreams to the host of a television show called *Live Your Dreams*, from a girl too insecure to talk to a handful of people to a woman standing on a stage speaking to thousands of entrepreneurs.

What will *not* reaching the point of having enough cost you?

Nobody can insist you make up your mind that you've had enough. Most of us wish we looked a different way, wore a different size, and weighed a few less pounds. But there comes a time when you step on the scale or look in the mirror and you see *that number* and you declare, "Okay, that's enough! Things are changing."

What about when you log into your bank account? What is *that number* that you see in your balance that causes you to become determined to make changes? What is *that number* of candles on the birthday cake that makes you realize they outnumber the accomplishments you've had? What does it take for you to have had enough?

Jim Rohn said that one of the emotions that can lead us to make quality decisions is disgust.[2] We normally don't equate the word *disgust* with positive action, but being disgusted with some aspect of your life can serve as vision and momentum to change. You become disgusted when you're tired of being embarrassed, ashamed, humiliated, and disappointed with where you are.

◦ ◦ ◦

You're reading this book because there is something in you that believes God has more for you. Something in you knows there is greatness on the inside waiting to be developed. Something in your spirit is intrigued by the possibility of achieving your biggest dreams.

A foodie friend of mine was watching a cooking competition show one night. The contestants had battled it out to make the best dish and win top prize. The woman who won a round of the competition got a major advantage for the next segment: a world-renowned chef came to her kitchen for ten minutes to help her create whatever she desired.

Something in you knows that there is greatness on the inside waiting to be developed.

The challenge was to make a spectacular dessert. Are you ready for this? The contestant's world-class chef just happened to be known for her pastries. Game over! You'd think that this woman had the challenge in the bag. We can prematurely announce the winner before the clock starts—or not.

The chef walked into the kitchen and asked what the contestant wanted her to do. Keep in mind, this is one of the best pastry chefs in the world. The contestant should have said, "What can you cook in under ten minutes that will help me win? Whatever you can cook, that's what I want." Just give the chef free rein in the kitchen!

Instead the contestant told the world-class chef to cut up fruit. The look on the chef's face said, "What?" The judges said, "What?!" I'm sure the TV viewers were screaming, "Are you nuts?" (As they threw bananas at the screen!)

The chef asked if the contestant was sure she just wanted fruit cut up, and the contestant confirmed that she had a recipe and only needed help with the fruit. That contestant lost the challenge. And she deserved to lose because she didn't use the greatness standing in her kitchen. She reduced the chef's expertise to slicing strawberries.

Well, God's Word says, "Greater is he that is in you, than he that is in the world" (1 John 4:4 KJV). Don't insult God by asking Him to do something small in your life. He is capable of so much more. But you need to ask Him for it. His Word says, "You do not have because you do not ask God" (James 4:2).

Don't diminish the greatness that is available in your life by asking God for small dreams. Call on Him to do what He does best. He is an expert in going beyond your wildest dreams. He specializes in doing the impossible.

I want to inspire you with this motivational story from the Bible of reaching the point of having had enough! In 2 Kings 7:3–10 we read about four men with leprosy who were sitting outside the gate of the city of Samaria while it was under siege from stronger enemies.

Until one day they'd had enough!

As they sat there thinking about their desperate situation, it dawned on them: "We're going to die from leprosy anyway. Or we could die going after our dream" (author's paraphrase).

One of those lepers said, "Are we just going to sit here until we die?" They did not know that they were twenty-four hours from the greatest miracle they had ever seen, but it required a decision. They got up! They decided to risk it all and go straight into the enemy camp, reasoning that they were going to die if they didn't do anything, so they might as well take a chance.

Little did they know that God "had caused the Arameans to hear the sound of chariots and horses and a great army" so that they all "ran for their lives" (2 Kings 7:6–7). When the lepers arrived, the entire enemy camp was vacated! They found gold, jewelry, money, clothing, and food beyond description.

Let me ask you today, Are you going to just sit here until you die? Are you going to let another year go by without deciding to change? Are you going to avoid alone time because it makes you uncomfortable? Are you going to stay busy, like those caterpillars, moving but not achieving anything? It's time to get fed up and start moving in the direction of your greatest potential.

Wilma Rudolph grew up with paralysis in her legs, and against all odds became a US Olympic Games winner of three gold medals in track and field. She was considered the "fastest woman in the world" in the 1960s, and in an interview said, "My doctor told me I would never walk again. My mother told me I would. I believed my mother."[3]

The world tells you your dream will never happen. God says it will. Believe God. Develop the greatness God has put in you!

CHAPTER 29

3 Decisions Successful People Make

The major mistake everyone makes is *waiting*!
Waiting for the right time. Waiting to feel motivated.
Waiting for someone to encourage you. It's
not coming! For the big stuff, for the hard stuff,
it requires a push, always has, always will!
—MEL ROBBINS

Emmy- and Grammy-winning actress Sarah Jessica Parker was born in Ohio. Her parents divorced when she was very young. Living in poverty, she grew up wearing ninety-nine-cent dresses. She was accustomed to living with little to nothing, surviving on welfare, and sometimes not having electricity, or skipping Christmas or birthdays. "The phone company would call and say, 'We're shutting your phones off.' And we were all old enough to either get the calls, or watch . . . my parents shuffling the money around."[1]

There was no way to hide her poverty. However, rather than focus on all the obstacles that could prevent her from her dream, she began looking for opportunities to change her life's direction and ultimately change her family's legacy.

This little girl with no advantages or favor on her side took responsibility for changing things. She got up and took action. She started practicing singing and studied ballet. The family moved from Cincinnati to New York City so she and her siblings could more easily get theater work. Behind closed doors, with nobody watching, she practiced and studied and seized opportunities to improve her craft.

In 1979 she made her Broadway debut at age fourteen as Annie in the legendary musical. One break led to another, and that little girl rose from severe poverty to sitcom sensation. Her net worth is now more than $200 million.[2]

Think of the hours Sarah Jessica Parker practiced her ballet poses, her dance moves, her voice lessons, and her lines to memorize. Nobody saw that little girl putting in the effort behind the scenes.[3] People are rewarded in public for what they practice in private.

Comfort and convenience run the lives of unsuccessful people. Successful people are always doing things that make them uncomfortable. The men and women in the Bible who literally changed the world were constantly taking big steps of faith outside their comfort zone! Peter walked on water. A widow gave the prophet Elisha her last bit of food during a famine. What do you need to do that makes you a little nervous, uncomfortable, awkward, and stretched? Do it.

> If you fall down, try to land on your back. As long as you can *look up*—you can *get up*!
> —LES BROWN

It could be that you need to go to a conference alone, go to dinner with someone who makes you nervous, send your manuscript to a publisher, agree to do an interview or to speak at an event, host a small group at your house, invite someone famous to speak at your event or church, sign up for a class, enroll at your local gym, agree to sing at the concert, sign up for a 5K, get your business cards printed—whatever it is, push yourself. Do it.

•   •   •

The Pool of Bethesda in Jerusalem was used for ritualistic baths, and it was also where people who were blind, paralyzed, or had other disabilities would go for healing. The first person to enter the water after it was stirred by an angel was healed (John 5:2–4).

Jesus visited this pool and noticed a man nearby who had been unable to walk for thirty-eight years. "When Jesus saw him lying there and learned that he had been in this condition for a long time, he asked him, '*Do you want to get well?*'" (verse 6).

Why would Jesus have to ask him if he wanted to get well? The man had been an invalid for *thirty-eight years*! Process the numbers. Nearly four decades. "The sick man answered Him, 'Sir, I have no man to put me into the pool when the water is stirred up; but while I am coming, another steps down before me'" (verse 7 NKJV).

Joyce Meyer explained that his response sounded like self-pity. He was waiting on someone else to come to his rescue and help him. Joyce humorously said, "In thirty-eight years, I could at least wiggle over to the pool and fall in!"[4]

In comparison, my question for you—and I had to answer this myself—is this:

Are you sure you want what you say you want?

Are you sure you want to be debt-free?

Are you sure you want to lose that weight?

Are you sure you want that job or promotion?

Are you sure you want to start a business or have your own ministry?

Are you sure you want to open a dance studio, daycare center, orphanage, or catering business? Because nothing has changed in five years, ten years, seventeen years, or even thirty-eight years.

In fact, listen to Jesus' response to this man who had been waiting to be healed for so long. You might imagine that He said something along the lines of, "Oh bless your heart. You have been through so much. Let me help you up and get you the proper care you need." No, in His heart of compassion, Jesus gave the man three commands:

1. Get up.
2. Pick up your bed.
3. Walk.

And He healed the man so he was able to obey. "Immediately the man was made well, took up his bed, and walked" (John 5:9 NKJV).

I'm going to use those three commands Jesus spoke to the man as the framework for talking about decisions successful people make.

1. Get Up

In other words, nobody can do this for you. You have to pick yourself up! You have to make the decision to not wait around another year feeling sorry for yourself, complaining about the conditions, and waiting for somebody to pick you up. Take responsibility for your life.

In the book *Maximum Achievement*, Brian Tracy said that there are three essentials for change: *wanting* to change, being *willing* to change, and being willing to expend *effort* for that change.[5]

John Assaraf and Murray Smith write that "by the time you're seventeen years old, you've heard, 'No, you can't,' an average of 150,000 times. You've heard, 'Yes, you can,' about 5,000 times. That's thirty nos for every yes."[6] That alone creates a belief system for keeping you stuck.

And that's why you must be very selective about who you allow to speak into your life. Remember: whoever has your *ear* has your life. When God tells you to step out in faith and go for that big dream, you will respond based on what your faith has been built on. Be intentional about listening to messages that build your faith. Keep building your faith muscle to *get up*!

2. Pick Up Your Bed

What does that mean? Stop wallowing around in that mess, that environment, those conditions that you've been lying in. Clean up your surroundings. Get rid of the junk from your past. You're no longer that person. You have a new identity, a new self-image, a new standard to uphold.

You know that *the way you do anything is the way you do everything*. You understand that your discipline in private is preparation for promotion in public. You understand that God sees everything, and when He spots a person of excellence, a person going the extra mile with nobody around, get ready—He's about to advance your life to a whole new level.

3. Walk

Walking is part of your body language. You walk differently when you have vision. You don't drag your feet and shuffle, head down, arms crossed, appearing lethargic, giving the impression that every step you take is draining you of energy.

No. You walk differently when you get inspired. A person with a vision, a goal, and a plan for their life walks faster. They have a destination in mind. They are focused. Anyone who is walking is going somewhere.

Remember, we move toward what we consistently see. You've got to see something to walk toward. You need to keep something in front of you that reminds you of your dream. If you can't see your vision, you're not moving toward it. Whatever you're dreaming about, keep it in front of you and start putting one foot in front of the other and start moving in the direction of your biggest dreams.

In comparison, what could Jesus be saying to *you* today?

Get up! *Pick up your music and sing!*
Get up! *Pick up your resume and get that dream job!*
Get up! *Pick up your passport and go on the trip!*
Get up! *Pick up your courage and open your business!*
Get up! *Pick up yourself and go to the gym!*
Get up! *Pick up your manuscript and write that book!*
Get up! *Pick up your journal and start listening!*

In other words, you must decide you've had enough.

Successful people decide to get up, pick up their beds, and walk toward their dreams. The Latin root for the word *decision* means "to cut off," as in cutting off alternative options.[7] For example, if you say, "I'll *try to* start getting up earlier" or "I'll *try to* build my own library" or "I'll *try to* set some goals," you haven't made a quality decision.

> Once I made a decision, I never thought about it again.
> —MICHAEL JORDAN

Have you ever put your big toe into a cold swimming pool? You have to decide if your plan is to slowly slide your whole foot in, then your ankles, your calves, and on up. Or do you just get the pain over with, take the plunge, and jump in full force?

The answer is, if you want to change your life, decide to jump in all the way!

CHAPTER 30

Get Your Obituary Ready!

Begin with the end in mind.
—STEPHEN COVEY

B ob Proctor filmed a video on the value of time, and I want to summarize his points. In the video he shows an hourglass full of sand. The grains of sand at the top represent the future. The bottom half of the hourglass represents the past. We know what's in our past and we can't do anything about it. The trick is that we don't know how much sand is left at the top of the hourglass because we can't see into the future. You may think you have a lot of time left, but you may have only a little. On the contrary, you may think you have only a little time but you have decades to live.

While explaining his view of time and the hourglass, Bob told a story about when he was young and was being raised by his grandmother. At sixty years old, she would say repeatedly, "One day, I'll be gone. I'll soon be home." She lived to be ninety-four years old. At age sixty she didn't think she had much time left, but she had more than three decades remaining to live her greatest dreams.

Bob also talked about a friend who at sixteen years old tragically died in a car accident. If you had asked that friend an hour before the wreck how much sand he thought he had left in his hourglass, he probably would have said, "At least half a century." But he didn't even have half an hour. We don't know how much sand we have left, but if you look at the hourglass, the sand is always moving.[1]

The psalmist David wrote, "Lord, remind me how brief my time on earth will be. Remind me that my days are numbered—how fleeting my life is" (Psalm 39:4 NLT). He also wrote, "I am here on earth for just a little while" (Psalm 119:19 GNT).

Joel Osteen said, "I can't think of anything more tragic than to come to the end of life on earth and realize that you have not really 'lived,' that you have not become what God created you to be. You simply endured an average, mediocre life. You got by, but you lived without passion or enthusiasm, allowing your inner potential to lie dormant and untapped."[2]

⁘

I want to tie a bow on this final chapter with a personal story that opened my eyes to the value of our limited time on earth. This tragedy impacted my life for more than four decades and helped me pinpoint my definition of success.

It was my junior year of high school in Crowley, Texas, when my English teacher, Mrs. Sawyer, had each of us do an assignment that was eerily life-changing.

"Class, I want you to get out a sheet of paper and write your full name at the top," said Mrs. Sawyer. "Underneath your name, write your birthdate and last night's date."

We all followed the instructions; however, we were totally unclear as to what this assignment had to do with diagramming sentences and reporting on current events.

Then she gave this chilling directive: "Now, I want each of you to write *your very own obituary*."

What? I thought, as the entire class of young, healthy seventeen-year-olds looked around at each other, completely confused and a little creeped out by this assignment.

"What would people say about you at your funeral?" Mrs. Sawyer bluntly asked. "Give it some thought. What would your parents say about you? How would your siblings describe you? How would your closest friends describe your personality? How did you spend your time? What were you known for? Were you friendly, rude, self-centered, giving, forgiving? Who did you help? What would your pastor say about you?"

After she got us thinking about these questions, she proceeded with this change in her directive: "Before you start, I don't want you to write what would be written up to this time in your life. I don't want you to write how your friends and family would currently describe you. I want you to write what you would like to be said about you at your funeral someday."

This awkward yet startling assignment was the result of a dear high school friend losing his life the night before. With mortality already at the forefront of our minds, there was a great sense of loss and sadness in the atmosphere on the school grounds. We were all at a loss for words and still in shock at his sudden, accidental death less than twelve hours before.

If a seventeen-year-old classmate could lose his life in a tragic, freak accident, what made us any different? What if that had been me who fell out of a truck and was run over on the school grounds? What stories would people be sharing about me this Friday morning?

My friend Paul didn't get another year, month, or even a day to make more decisions. He only had the short seventeen years he was given on earth to live the best way possible, and I'm glad to say, he did.

This assignment was more than thought provoking; it was life-changing, destiny pointing, and discipline activating. More than thirty-five years later, I still think about English class that October morning.

As we completed our assignment, Mrs. Sawyer held out her hand to collect the obituaries and said, "Students, you have not only written your obituaries, but you've also written your dreams. Now go live them." Wow! What a profound and life-altering assignment. And it's not for high school students alone; it's for anyone who wants to live a life designed to succeed on purpose. It's for anyone who longs to make the years matter and the days count. It's for you today to trigger self-motivation.

, , ,

When you come to the end of your life and you look back, what do you want people to say about you? How would they describe you? What would they say you did during your time on earth? Did you make a difference in anyone's life? Were you focused on making an impact? Did you block out the time to truly hear God speak wisdom for your journey? Did you do all the things you said you would do? Did you live a full life? Did you have a vision before you? Did you fully enjoy the value of each day?

Or did you live a life of regret—visionless, going through the motions without much thought about your purpose? Did you waste days watching television, gossiping, scrolling through social media for countless hours, pushing the snooze button, and letting opportunities pass you by?

Twenty years after that high school assignment, I returned to it as I sat at my keyboard and began writing my new, revised obituary as a full-grown woman, wife, mother, and leader. I sat alone in my guest bedroom in 2006 with nothing but a laptop and a head full of questions, ideas, thoughts, and dreams. I wrote my full name at the top with my birthdate underneath—but no "expiration date" attached. I began writing exactly how I wanted to be remembered as a person, a wife, a mother, a daughter, a friend, a leader, and a world changer.

I wrote big, audacious, crazy, out-of-the-realm-of-possibility paragraphs that sent questions to my mind immediately: *How in the world—?* and *Who do you think you are?* But I didn't let that stop me from dreaming. I let my imagination soar and my aspirations exceed what I was currently capable of doing.

Something remarkable happened. It caused a flame in me to ignite and come alive unlike any other exercise I had ever done. It was a completely different mental challenge than just writing down my goals for the year of paying off debts and losing five pounds. When you imagine coming to the end of your life and your closest family and friends are describing how you lived, hopefully they'll say more than that you finally paid off that student loan! The exercise will awaken dreams in you that you never thought possible.

> I let my imagination soar and my aspirations exceed what I was currently capable of doing.

What you're doing, in essence, is defining success for *you*. As creepy as it sounds, you're writing what you want printed in black and white on the back pages of your local—or global—newspaper for all the world to read. Why not write something that inspires others to get up off the couch, make a difference with their lives, and truly live their definition of success?

. . .

Years before I was living my dreams, I was driving to work and practicing these private habits we've discussed, listening to a faith-building message during my commute. Suddenly I heard a statement that shook me up: *Somebody in need is waiting on the other side of your obedience.* The minister said it twice and then the audio ended. *Somebody in need is waiting on the other side of your obedience.*

As those words replayed in my head, with my hands on the wheel and my eyes staring at the road in front of me, I questioned, "Could somebody really be waiting on *me* to get my act together? Is anybody waiting on me to get up earlier in the mornings, to read, to journal, to set goals, to be grateful? No. I doubt it."

And I finished my drive to work. But I continued hearing those words in my head, and that led to continuing to get up each morning, invest in myself, listen, journal, dream, and push myself out of my comfort zone.

Today I get to hear stories or meet people like the tall man in Seattle who approached me during a book signing with tears rolling down his face and simply asked for a hug. Of course I obliged. We took a group picture with his family and before they walked away, his daughter came back to me and said, "You'll never know what that hug and what this ministry means to our family! My dad refused to go to church with us for years. He was depressed, an alcoholic, near suicidal, and wanted *nothing* to do with God! He stumbled across you on YouTube and gave his heart to the Lord. He stopped drinking, he's a completely different person, and he told the family, 'Terri is in Seattle this weekend. We have to go hear her!' He's not just a fan, he's a fanatic about Jesus."

I can't help but think:

> *What if I had slept in those extra thirty minutes thinking it's not that big a deal?*
> *What if I had continued watching that show instead of reading a book?*
> *What if I had disregarded those two words,* clean up, *because there's no way that could be the voice of God?*
> *What if I gave up on those goals because they took longer than twelve months to achieve?*

I want you to know that God sees everything. All those mornings you force yourself to get up early and exercise while everyone else sleeps in, you're preparing. For each lunch break when you read an encouraging book instead of wasting time scrolling through social media, you're getting ready. In every commute spent listening to a motivational podcast, you're going above average. It is gearing you up for greatness. Preparation time is never wasted time.

Who could be waiting on you? Who is on the other side of your obedience? Whose life will be impacted because you spent time alone, got silent, developed the ten success habits in private, and God was able to promote you in public?

Years ago John Maxwell was given a book titled *The Greatest Story Ever Told*. He loved to read and thought, *Wow, what a title!* When he opened it up, much to his surprise, all the pages were blank. He asked, "It says the greatest story ever told? There's nothing here."

He was told to look at the first page. He flipped to the front where he saw, "Dear John, your life is before you. Fill these pages with your dreams, your hopes, your desires, and make it the greatest story ever told." John took the book home with him and started writing that very day. On the first page he wrote, "I want to make a difference."[3]

And that's the same way that an insecure, rejected, lonely young girl scribbling "I want to die" became a successful woman, wife, and mother penning how she wants to live—all within the pages of a simple notebook.

It's your turn. Grab your journal. Close the door. And start listening. If you want to know where your life is headed, time *alone* will tell. "Your Father, who sees what is done in secret, will reward you" (Matthew 6:4).

Behind-the-Scenes Habits
That Drive Crazy Success

HABIT #10

Get up, pick up your dream, and start walking toward it. It's the alone advantage that leads to fulfilling your life assignment—while greatly impacting someone in need.

> So let's keep focused on that goal, those of us who want everything God has for us. If any of you have something else in mind, something less than total commitment, God will clear your blurred vision—you'll see it yet! Now that we're on the right track, let's stay on it.
> —PHILIPPIANS 3:15–16 MSG

Notes

Introduction

1. *The Oxford Pocket Dictionary of Current English*, s.v. "advantage," Encyclopedia.com, updated June 11, 2018, https://www.encyclopedia .com/humanities/dictionaries-thesauruses-pictures-and-press-releases /advantage-0.
2. Attributed online to Tony Robbins, but origin is uncertain.
3. Carmine Gallo, "Richard Branson: If It Can't Fit on the Back of an Envelope, It's Rubbish (An Interview)," *Forbes*, October 22, 2012, https://www.forbes.com/sites/carminegallo/2012/10/22/richard -branson-if-it-cant-fit-on-the-back-of-an-envelope-its-rubbish -interview/.
4. Robin Sharma, "How to Be Comfortable Being Alone," published by Robin Sharma on April 4, 2019, YouTube video, 12:34, https://youtu .be/oLxafxniWZc.
5. Joyce Meyer, *Change Your Words, Change Your Life: Understanding the Power of Every Word You Speak* (New York: Faith Words, 2012).

Chapter 1: Hear the Music

1. Gene Weingarten, "Pearls Before Breakfast: Can One of the Nation's Great Musicians Cut Through the Fog of a DC Rush Hour? Let's Find Out," *Washington Post*, September 23, 2014, https://www .washingtonpost.com/lifestyle/magazine/pearls-before-breakfast-can -one-of-the-nations-great-musicians-cut-through-the-fog-of-a-dc-rush -hour-lets-find-out/2014/09/23/8a6d46da-4331–11e4-b47c -f5889e061e5f_story.html.
2. Weingarten, "Pearls Before Breakfast."
3. Bob Beaudine, *2 Chairs: The Secret That Changes Everything* (Franklin, TN: Worthy Publishing, 2016), 11.

4. Carmine Gallo, *The Storyteller's Secret: From TED Speakers to Business Legends, Why Some Ideas Catch On and Others Don't* (New York: St. Martin's, 2016), 164.
5. Gallo, *Storyteller's Secret*, 164.
6. John Maxwell, *How Successful People Think: Change Your Thinking, Change Your Life* (New York: Center Street, 2009), xiii.
7. "Keyword Search: Meditate," Bible Gateway, accessed August 15, 2023, https://www.biblegateway.com/quicksearch/?quicksearch =meditate&version=NIV.
8. Michael Todd, *Crazy Faith: It's Only Crazy Until It Happens* (New York: Waterbrook, 2021), 104.

Chapter 2: 5 Things Successful People Write in Their Journals

1. Jim Rohn, "Keeping a Journal," Get Motivation, accessed June 2, 2023, https://www.getmotivation.com/jimrohn/jim-rohn-keeping-a -journal.html.
2. Jack Canfield, *The Success Principles: How to Get From Where You Are to Where You Want to Be*, 10th anniversary ed. (New York: William Morrow, 2015), 385.
3. Minte Studio, "5 Celebrities Who Keep a Journal," Medium, July 23, 2018, https://medium.com/@mintestudio/5-celebrities-who-keep-a -journal-a6888bc2a42b.
4. Minte Studio, "5 Celebrities Who Keep a Journal."
5. Gary Keller, *The ONE Thing: The Surprisingly Simple Truth About Extraordinary Results* (Portland, OR: Bard Press, 2013), chap. 10.
6. "Journaling Your Thoughts and Feelings," Lifeline, accessed August 30, 2023, https://toolkit.lifeline.org.au/articles/techniques /journaling-your-thoughts-and-feelings.
7. Amy Purdy, "Living Beyond Limits," TED, May 2011, transcript, https://www.ted.com/talks/amy_purdy_living_beyond_limits /transcript?language=en.
8. Carmine Gallo, *The Storyteller's Secret: From TED Speakers to Business Legends, Why Some Ideas Catch On and Others Don't* (New York: St. Martin's, 2016), 170.
9. Gallo, *Storyteller's Secret*, 170–71.

Chapter 3: Get Serious Behind Closed Doors

1. Lisa Nichols with Tom Bilyeu, "Rescue Yourself Overcome Fear—Find Success Serving Others (IQ #66)," published by Mindset Persistence on November 4, 2019, YouTube video, 55:14, https://www.youtube.com/watch?v=PPRaL40IAdI.
2. "Lisa Nichols," Motivating the Masses, accessed June 6, 2023, https://motivatingthemasses.com/about/lisa-nichols/.
3. T. L. Osborn, quoted in Jerry Savelle, "Never Stop Dreaming," *Jerry Savelle Ministries International* (July–September 2017), 6, PDF, https://www.jerrysavelle.org/downloads/AIF/2017-AIF-Jul-Sep.pdf.
4. Richard Feloni, "Why Richard Branson Never Goes Anywhere Without a Notebook," Yahoo! News, September 15, 2014, https://www.yahoo.com/news/why-richard-branson-never-goes-145946207.html.
5. Greg McKeown, "One Surprising Secret of Highly Productive People," LinkedIn, March 31, 2014, https://www.linkedin.com/pulse/20140331090432–8353952-one-surprisingly-secret-of-highly-productive-people/.
6. "Investing Basics," Retire in Progress, August 23, 2016, https://retireinprogress.com/investing/.
7. *Collins English Dictionary*, s.v. "invest," accessed June 6, 2023, https://www.collinsdictionary.com/us/dictionary/english/invest.

Chapter 4: Your Laundry Isn't Finished

1. Joyce Meyer, "Put It Back!," published by Joyce Meyer Ministries on September 23, 2022, Facebook video, 3:05, https://www.facebook.com/joycemeyerministries/videos/put-it-back/808054607017058/.
2. Suzanne Evans, *The Way You Do Anything Is the Way You Do Everything: The Why of Why Your Business Isn't Making More Money* (Hoboken, NJ: Wiley, 2014).
3. William H. McRaven, quoted in Liberty Hardy, "The Best Inspirational Quotes from Make Your Bed by Admiral McRaven," Hachette Book Group, accessed June 2, 2023, https://www.hachettebookgroup.com/articles/best-inspirational-quotes-from-make-your-bed/.
4. *Roget's Twenty-First Century Thesaurus*, 3rd ed., s.v. "preferred," Thesaurus.com, accessed June 6, 2023, https://www.thesaurus.com/browse/preferred.

Chapter 5: 10 Reasons Successful People Are Organized

1. Julie Harvey, "What Does Your Disorganization Say About You?," The SpaceMaster Speaks, February 7, 2011, https://thespacemaster .wordpress.com/2011/02/07/what-does-your-disorganization-say -about-you/.

2. "Home Organization Is a Major Source of Stress for Americans, Survey Finds," HuffPost, May 22, 2013, https://www.huffpost.com /entry/home-organization-stress-survey_n_3308575.

3. Kathryn Schultz, "When Things Go Missing," *New Yorker*, February 5, 2017, https://www.newyorker.com/magazine/2017/02/13 /when-things-go-missing.

4. Pixie Technology Inc., "Lost and Found: The Average American Spends 2.5 Days Each Year Looking for Lost Items Collectively Costing U.S. Households $2.7 Billion Annually in Replacement Costs," Cision Newswire, May 2, 2017, https://www.prnewswire.com /news-releases/lost-and-found-the-average-american-spends-25-days -each-year-looking-for-lost-items-collectively-costing-us-households -27-billion-annually-in-replacement-costs-300449305.html.

5. Daryl Austin, "Stress Overload? Survey Says Get Organized," *Forbes*, September 6, 2021, https://www.forbes.com/sites/darylaustin/2021 /09/06/stress-overload-survey-says-get-organized/?sh=22411bbd52dd; Joseph Staples, "Nearly Two-Thirds of Adults Want to Become More Organized Post Pandemic," SWNS Digital, October 4, 2021, https:// swnsdigital.com/us/2021/06/nearly-two-thirds-of-americans-want-to -become-more-organized-post-pandemic/.

6. UPMC Western Behavioral Health, "What's the Connection Between Clutter and Stress?," UPMC Health Beat, February 18, 2021, https:// share.upmc.com/2021/02/clutter-and-stress/.

7. Matthew Clark, "How Decluttering Your Space Could Make You Healthier and Happier," Mayo Clinic, May 20, 2021, https://www .mayoclinic.org/healthy-lifestyle/stress-management/in-depth/how -decluttering-your-space-could-make-you-healthier-and-happier /art-20390064.

8. Deane Alban, "Remove Clutter to Reduce Stress (+ 5-Step Decluttering System)," Be Brain Fit, last updated March 7, 2022, https://bebrainfit.com/clutter-stress/.

Chapter 6: Get Your 20-Minute Timer

1. Brian Tracy, *Maximum Achievements: Strategies and Skills That Will Unlock Your Hidden Powers to Succeed* (New York: Simon & Schuster, 1993), 55.
2. Michael J. Formica, "How the Environment We Create Is a Reflection of Our State of Mind," *Psychology Today*, July 29, 2008, https://www.psychologytoday.com/us/blog/enlightened-living/200807/how-the-environment-we-create-is-a-reflection-of-our-state-of-mind.
3. Amanda Enayati, "Why Clutter Matters and Decluttering Is Difficult," Yahoo! News, June 25, 2012, https://www.yahoo.com/news/blogs/spaces/why-clutter-matters-decluttering-difficult-232127340.html.
4. John C. Maxwell, *Today Matters: 12 Daily Practices to Guarantee Tomorrow's Success* (New York: Hatchette, 2004), 18, 19.

Chapter 7: You Can Conquer the Covers

1. Walter Isaacson, *Benjamin Franklin: An American Life* (New York: Simon & Schuster, 2004), 98.
2. Terri Savelle Foy, "Change Your Life," *Adventures in Faith* (July–September 2021), 21, PDF, https://www.jerrysavelle.org/images/2021/07/JulySeptember2021.pdf; Jon Acuff, *Quitter: Closing the Gap Between Your Day Job & Your Dream* (Brentwood, TN: Ramsey Press, 2011).
3. Zig Ziglar, *See You at the Top*, 25th anniversary ed. (Gretna, LA: Pelican Publishing, 2000), 238.
4. Harriet Brown, "The Weight of the Evidence," *Slate*, March 24, 2015, https://slate.com/technology/2015/03/diets-do-not-work-the-thin-evidence-that-losing-weight-makes-you-healthier.html.
5. Jim Rohn, "Rohn: Being Successful Is a Choice," *Success*, October 1, 2016, https://www.success.com/rohn-being-successful-is-a-personal-choice/.

Chapter 8: 5 Things Successful People Do Before Breakfast

1. Michael Todd, *Crazy Faith: It's Only Crazy Until It Happens* (New York: Waterbrook, 2021), 103.
2. Robert J. Morgan, *Mastering Life Before It's Too Late: 10 Biblical Strategies for a Lifetime of Purpose* (New York: Howard Books, 2016), 113.

3. Morgan, *Mastering Life*, 113.

4. Kobe Bryant, "The Power of Sleep & Meditation," published by Thrive on January 27, 2020, YouTube video, 5:56, https://www.youtube.com/watch?v=LdrVVJPlUK4.

5. Sarah Akida, "Famous People Who Meditate," Mettitation, accessed June 6, 2023, https://www.mettitation.com/meditationblog/famous-people-who-meditate; Melissa Wozniak, "50 Famous People Who Meditate," Meditation Wise, accessed June 7, 2023, https://www.meditationwise.com/50-famous-people-who-meditate; Diana Price, "Gratitude and Grace: The Sheryl Crow Interview," Hematology Oncology Associates of Fredricksburg, 2016, https://www.hoafredericksburg.com/gratitude-and-grace-the-sheryl-crow-interview/; "Steve Harvey's Daily Routine: How He Maintains Health and Energy," L'evate You, accessed June 7, 2023, https://levateyou.com/blogs/lab/steve-harvey-daily-routine.

6. Jack Canfield, "3 Mentors of My Life Who Changed Everything," published by Jack Canfield on April 14, 2022, YouTube video, 8:27, https://www.youtube.com/watch?v=EbhslGQMH24&t=36s.

7. Gail Matthews, "Goal Research Summary" (paper, Dominican University, San Rafael, CA, February 2020), https://dominican.edu/sites/default/files/2020–02/gailmatthews-harvard-goals-researchsummary.pdf.

8. Tony Robbins, "Empowering Quotes from Tony Robbins," Tony Robbins (website), accessed June 7, 2023, https://www.tonyrobbins.com/tony-robbins-quotes/.

9. Benjamin Svetkey, "Emma Stone's Battle with Shyness, Panic Attacks and Phobias on the Way to the Oscars," *Hollywood Reporter*, January 26, 2017, https://www.hollywoodreporter.com/movies/movie-features/emma-stones-battle-shyness-panic-attacks-phobias-way-oscars-968543/.

10. James Clear, "How Long Does It Actually Take to Form a New Habit? (Backed by Science)," James Clear (website), accessed August 30, 2023, https://jamesclear.com/new-habit.

11. John Assaraf (@johnassarafpage), "The Only Way to Stop Procrastinating," Facebook video, streamed live on June 15, 2021, https://www.facebook.com/johnassarafpage/videos/the-only-way-to-stop-procrastinating/1151256722055535/.

12. George S. James, "Chapter 3: A Background of Memories of Working with Dr. Wernher von Braun, Krafft Ehricke and Members of the Peenemünde Group" (paper presented at the Forty-Eighth History Symposium of the International Academy of Astronautics, Toronto, September 29–October 4, 2014), 33, PDF, https://www.academia.edu/21025322/V46_Chapter_3text.

Chapter 9: Get Your Day Planned Before Bedtime

1. Zig Ziglar, *Selling 101: What Every Successful Sales Professional Needs to Know* (Nashville: HarperCollins Leadership, 2003), 35–36.
2. Julie Morgenstern, *Time Management from the Inside Out* (New York: Henry Holt and Company, 2004), 105.
3. Terry Goodrich, "Can Writing Your 'To-Do's' Help You to Doze? Baylor Study Suggests Jotting Down Tasks Can Speed the Trip to Dreamland," Baylor University, January 11, 2018, https://news.web.baylor.edu/news/story/2018/can-writing-your-dos-help-you-doze-baylor-study-suggests-jotting-down-tasks-can.
4. Piyush Sharma, "A Financial Planner Interviewed 233 Rich People and Here Is What He Found Out," MensXP, May 14, 2018, https://www.mensxp.com/work-life/finance/44785-a-financial-planner-interviewed-233-rich-people-here-is-what-he-found-out.html.
5. James Clear, "The 5 Triggers That Make a Habit Stick," James Clear (website), accessed June 21, 2023, https://jamesclear.com/habit-triggers.
6. John C. Maxwell, *Make Today Count* (New York: Hatchette, 2004), 19.
7. Dixie Cartwright, "Why Do Successful People Wake Up Early?," Mississippi State University, August 21, 2019, http://ce.extension.msstate.edu/node/740.

Chapter 10: You Can't Have the Marshmallow

1. Dr. Seuss, *I Can Read with My Eyes Shut!* (New York: Random House, 1978), 27.
2. Erik Hamre, "How Kobe Outworked the Rest to Go from Summer League Failure to 5x NBA Champion," Medium, March 8, 2020, https://medium.com/skilluped/how-kobe-outworked-the-rest-to-go-from-summer-league-failure-to-5x-nba-champion-773602807e71.

3. David Angstadt, "Bigger Than Basketball—The Legacy of Kobe Bryant," LinkedIn, February 4, 2020, https://www.linkedin.com /pulse/bigger-than-basketball-legacy-kobe-bryant-david-angstadt/.

4. Eric Eulau, "Lakers: Kobe Bryant and His GOAT Mountain," FanNation, February 18, 2022, https://www.si.com/nba/lakers/news /lakers-kobe-bryant-and-his-goat-mountain-ee21.

5. Napoleon Hill Foundation (@NapoleaonHillFoundation), Facebook photo post, July 31, 2017, https://m.facebook.com/NapoleonHill Foundation/photos/the-person-who-stops-studying-merely-because -he-has-finished-school-is-forever-h/10155536838082138/.

6. Zig Ziglar, *See You at the Top*, 25th anniversary ed. (Gretna, LA: Pelican Publishing, 2000), 241, 246.

7. Amy Watson, "Average Daily Time Spent Reading Per Capita in the United States from 2014 to 2021 (In Hours)," Statista, August 3, 2022, https://www.statista.com/statistics/622525/time-reading-us/.

8. Mike Van Hoozer, "How Ralph Waldo Emerson Helped Me Understand My Calling," Mike Van Hoozer (website), accessed June 7, 2023, https://mikevanhoozer.com/emerson-and-my-calling/.

9. Tim Grover, "The Body Has Limitations the Mind Does Not," published by Hedi El Abed on July 30, 2017, YouTube video, 2:06, https://www.youtube.com/watch?v=3q9GvQVGNVA.

10. Angel E. Navidad, "Marshmallow Test Experiment and Delayed Gratification," Simply Psychology, updated May 1, 2023, https:// www.simplypsychology.org/marshmallow-test.html.

Chapter 11: What Successful People Do In Traffic

1. "How to Get Out of a Car Loan," Ramsey Solutions, May 30, 2023, https://www.ramseysolutions.com/debt/dont-let-your-car-loan-own -you.

2. Tom Corley, "I Spent 5 Years Interviewing 233 Millionaires— Here Are the 6 Habits That Made Them Ultra Wealthy," CNBC, October 9, 2022, https://www.cnbc.com/2022/10/09/i-spent-5-year -interviewing-233-millionaires-here-are-the-habits-that-made-them -rich-and-successful.html.

3. Excerpts from preaching by my dad, Jerry Savelle.

4. "Census Bureau Estimates Show Average One-Way Travel Time to Work Rises to All-Time High," United States Census Bureau, last

updated October 8, 2021, https://www.census.gov/newsroom/press
-releases/2021/one-way-travel-time-to-work-rises.html.

5. Erin Dooley, "Here's How Much Time Americans Waste in Traffic,"
ABC News, August 25, 2015, https://abcnews.go.com/US/time
-americans-waste-traffic/story?id=33313765.

6. Chris Gilligan, "U.S. Cities with the Worst Traffic," *U.S. News &
World Report*, May 24, 2023, https://www.usnews.com/news/cities
/articles/10-cities-with-the-worst-traffic-in-the-us.

7. John Wooden, quoted in Craig Impelman, "If You Are Through
Learning, You Are Through," The Wooden Effect, October 30,
2019, https://www.thewoodeneffect.com/if-you-are-through-learning
-you-are-through/.

Chapter 12: Get Your Library Started

1. Jim Rohn, "Jim Rohn, Part 2," posted by Mind fed (@mind.fed) on
November 10, 2021, TikTok video, 1:31, https://www.tiktok.com
/@mind.fed/video/7029037280140561665.

2. John C. Maxwell (@TheJohnCMaxwell), Twitter post, January 13,
2018, 10:45 p.m., https://twitter.com/TheJohnCMaxwell/status
/952401159033098240.

3. Thomas Stanley, *The Millionaire Next Door: Secrets to America's
Wealthy* (1996; repr., New York: Taylor Trade Publishing, 2010), xiv.

4. Brian Tracy, *No Excuses! The Power of Self-Discipline* (New York:
Vanguard Press, 2010), 90–92.

Chapter 13: Can You Imagine?

1. Charles Duhigg, *The Power of Habit: Why We Do What We Do in Life
and Business* (New York: Random House, 2012), 111.

2. Michael Todd, *Crazy Faith: It's Only Crazy Until It Happens* (New
York: Waterbrook, 2021), 25.

3. Steve Harvey, *Act Like a Success, Think Like a Success: Discovering Your
Gift and the Way to Life's Riches* (New York: Amistad, 2014), 52–53.

4. John C. Maxwell, *Be All You Can Be: A Challenge to Stretch Your
God-Given Potential* (1987; repr., Colorado Springs, CO: David C.
Cook, 2007), 64–65.

5. Brian Tracy (@BrianTracyPage), "Practice 'back from the future'
thinking," Facebook photo post, December 23, 2013, https://www

.facebook.com/BrianTracyPage/photos/a.454285253459/10151898097
083460/?type=3.

6. Maxwell, *Be All You Can Be*, 56.

7. James Clear (@JamesClear), Twitter post, August 1, 2020, 8:29 p.m.,
https://twitter.com/JamesClear/status/1289735091741052929.

8. Billy Cox, "Clarity Is Power: The Importance of Setting Clear Goals,"
Blog Billy, April 24, 2023, https://billycox.com/clarity-is-power-the
-importance-of-setting-clear-goals/.

Chapter 14: 7 Indicators Successful People Use to Validate Their Dreams

1. George Sumner, "Sting: How I Started Writing Songs Again," TED,
2014, https://www.ted.com/talks/sting_how_i_started_writing
_songs_again?language=en, quoted in Carmine Gallo, *The Storyteller's
Secret: From TED Speakers to Business Legends, Why Some Ideas Catch
On and Others Don't* (New York: St. Martin's Press, 2016), 30–31.

2. Dolly Parton, "Dolly's Tin Can and Tobacco Stick Microphone,"
Dolly Parton Productions, last updated October 15, 2020, https://
dollyparton.com/life-and-career/a-tin-can-and-a-tobacco-stick/9740.

3. Box Office Mojo, "Top Lifetime Grosses," IMDb, last updated June 8,
2023, https://www.boxofficemojo.com/chart/top_lifetime_gross/?area
=XWW.

4. John Broadway, "8 Ways Kobe Lives on Through Me," Medium,
January 26, 2022, https://medium.com/age-of-awareness/8-ways-kobe
-lives-on-through-me-d4197ce8fcc9.

5. Bob Guccione Jr., "Mississippi Calling," *Garden & Gun*, February
/March 2012, https://gardenandgun.com/feature/mississippi-calling/.

6. Simon Hattenstone, "Shania Twain on Abuse, Betrayal and Finding
Her Voice: 'I Wanted a Break—But Not for 15 Years,'" *The Guardian*,
April 22, 2018, https://www.theguardian.com/music/2018/apr/22
/shania-twain-unexpected-return-freak-illness-country-pop-star.

7. Dale Carnegie, "Being Discouraged Never Pays," *Marshall News
Messenger*, January 29, 1942, 6.

8. Scott Beggs, "How Star Wars Began: As an Indie Film No Studio
Wanted to Make," *Vanity Fair*, December 18, 2015, https://www
.vanityfair.com/hollywood/2015/12/star-wars-george-lucas
-independent-film.

9. George Lucas, "George Lucas: Cinematic Phenomenon," Academy of Achievement, February 7, 2022, https://achievement.org/achiever/george-lucas/.

10. "Star Wars: How George Lucas Made the Movie Nobody Believed In," Goalcast, accessed August 16, 2023, https://www.goalcast.com/george-lucas-star-wars-making-masterpiece/.

11. Lucas, "George Lucas."

12. "Milton Hershey and His Chocolate Factory," Reading Is Fundamental, accessed August 16, 2023, https://www.rif.org/literacy-central/reading-experience/milton-hershey-and-his-chocolate-factory-easy.

13. Bill Purvis, *Make a Break for It: Unleashing the Power of Personal and Spiritual Growth* (Grand Rapids: Zondervan, 2016), 89.

Chapter 15: Get Your Vision Board in the Right Spot

1. Steve Chandler, *This Book Will Motivate You: 100 Ways to Kickstart Your Life Goals* (Newburyport, MA: Career Press, 2023), 89.

2. Steve Harvey (@SteveHarvey), "My vision board is on my iPhone," Facebook photo, January 28, 2016, https://www.facebook.com/SteveHarvey/photos/a.1401267026800825/1659165181011007/.

3. "Jeff Probst," Television Academy Foundation: The Interviews, accessed August 17, 2023, streaming video, 59:27, https://interviews.televisionacademy.com/interviews/jeff-probst?clip=2, quoted in "Jeff Probst," Survivor Wiki, accessed August 17, 2023, https://survivor.fandom.com/wiki/Jeff_Probst.

4. Joe Reid, "The Best 20 Reality Shows of All Time," *Variety*, December 22, 2021, https://variety.com/lists/best-reality-shows-of-all-time-ranked/the-real-world/.

5. Brian Tracy, "The 7 Cs to Success," published by LifeVantage on August 1, 2019, YouTube video, https://www.youtube.com/watch?v=FfohcP_zBkQ.

6. *Oxford English Dictionary*, s.v. "meditate," accessed August 17, 2023, https://www.oed.com/dictionary/meditate_v?tab=factsheet#37553530.

7. *Merriam-Webster*, s.v. "reflect," accessed August 17, 2023, https://www.merriam-webster.com/dictionary/reflect.

Chapter 16: What Are You Doing New Year's Eve?

1. Whatmeworry, "Have You Heard of the French Caterpillar Experiment?," HardwareZone Forums, August 30, 2022, https:// forums.hardwarezone.com.sg/threads/have-you-heard-of-the-french -caterpillar-experiment.6802108/.
2. Zig Ziglar, "The Lack of Time is Not Your Problem!," publised by The Outcome on September 23, 2020, YouTube video, 6:43, https:// www.youtube.com/watch?v=0kPfOCZTuKY.
3. Brian Tracy, "How to Set Long-Term Goals for Success in Business," Brian Tracy International, accessed August 17, 2023, https://www .briantracy.com/blog/business-success/long-term-goals/.
4. Brian Scudamore, "WTF?! (Willing to Fail): Brian Scudamore," November 7, 2018, on *Author Hour*, produced by Charlie Hoehn, transcript, https://authorhour.co/wtf-willing-fail-brian-scudamore/.
5. John von Saders, "Effectuation Case Study: 1–800-GOT-JUNK?," Medium, July 12, 2022, https://blog.startupstash.com/effectuation -case-study-1–800-got-junk-1fd89c0ac165.

Chapter 17: 7 Tips Successful People Use to Set Goals

1. "49 Celebrities with Surprisingly Ordinary Pre-Fame Jobs," Love Inc., October 27, 2017, https://www.loveinc.com/gallerylist/68835/49 -celebrities-with-surprisingly-ordinary-prefame-jobs.
2. Michael Hyatt, "5 Reasons Why You Should Commit Your Goals to Writing," Full Focus, October 20, 2022, https://fullfocus.co/5 -reasons-why-you-should-commit-your-goals-to-writing/.
3. Dixie Gillaspie, "You'll Never Accomplish Goals You Don't Really Care About," *Entrepreneur*, January 20, 2017, https://www .entrepreneur.com/living/youll-never-accomplish-goals-you-dont -really-care-about/254371.
4. "New Year's Resolution Statistics (2022 Updated)," Discover Happy Habits, updated August 22, 2022, https://discoverhappyhabits.com /new-years-resolution-statistics/#resolutions-success-failure.
5. Brad Zomick, "Top 10 Most Common New Year's Resolutions (And How to Follow Through on Them)," Go Skills, accessed August 17, 2023, https://www.goskills.com/Soft-Skills/Resources/Top-10-new -years-resolutions.
6. Ben K., "Brian Tracy's '10x10' (Goal Setting Method)," LinkedIn,

February 8, 2021, https://www.linkedin.com/pulse/brian-tracys-10x10
-goal-setting-method-ben-kirk/.
7. John Chancellor, "The Study of 4,000," Teach the Soul, May 10,
2021, http://www.teachthesoul.com/2021/05/the-study-of-4000/.

Chapter 18: Get Comfortable Saying No

1. Marcel Schwantes, "Warren Buffett Says This 1 Simple Habit
Separates Successful People from Everyone Else," *Inc.*, August 11,
2023, https://www.inc.com/jenna-anderson/3-ways-to-successfully
-expand-your-business-internationally.html.
2. Walter Isaacson, *Steve Jobs* (New York: Simon & Schuster, 2011), 360.
3. David Feldman, *How Does Aspirin Find a Headache?* (New York:
HarperCollins, 1993), 9–11.
4. Dave Ramsey, *The Total Money Makeover Classic Edition: A Proven
Plan for Success* (Nashville: Thomas Nelson, 2013).
5. John Maxwell, *The 15 Invaluable Laws of Growth*, 10th anniversary
ed. (New York: Center Street, 2022), 112.

Chapter 19: Be Your Own Cheerleader

1. As of September 2023, Selena Gomez had 428.5 million Instagram
followers, the most of any woman, according to HypeAuditor, https://
hypeauditor.com/instagram/selenagomez/.
2. Christal Yuen, "Selena Gomez Reveals Lifesaving Kidney Transplant
to Bring Awareness to Lupus," Healthline, August 20, 2018, https://
www.healthline.com/health/lupus/selena-gomez-kidney-transplant
-lupus.
3. Bolono Sekudo, "Selena Gomez Works on Her Self-Confidence
Daily and 'I Am Enough' Is Her Favourite Affirmation," News24,
February 4, 2022, https://www.news24.com/life/archive/selena
-gomez-works-on-her-self-confidence-daily-and-i-am-enough-is
-her-favourite-affirmation-20220204.
4. Steve Harvey, *Act Like a Success, Think Like a Success:
Discovering Your Gift and the Way to Life's Riches* (New York:
Amistad, 2014), 22.
5. Christina Garibaldi, "This Is Why Ed Sheeran Won't Hook Up with
Taylor Swift," MTV, May 29, 2015, https://www.mtv.com
/news/95c842/ed-sheeran-taylor-swift-hook-up-katy-perry.

6. Brenton Blanchet, "Ed Sheeran Says He 'Cured' His Stutter by Rapping Along to Eminem's 'The Marshall Mathers LP,'" *People*, May 15, 2023, https://people.com/music/ed-sheeran-says-his-stutter-was-cured-by-rapping-eminems-marshall-mathers-lp/.

7. "Ed Sheeran," *Billboard*, accessed August 17, 2023, https://www.billboard.com/artist/ed-sheeran/.

8. James Clear, *Atomic Habits* (New York: Avery, 2018), 32.

9. Pete Weishaupt, "Behavior Before Success," Medium, June 2, 2020, https://peteweishaupt.medium.com/behavior-before-success-5c7fa26a5732, quoting from Tom Bilyeu, "How to Break the Addiction to Negative Thoughts and Emotions in 31 Minutes: Trevor Moawad," published by Tom Bilyeu on March 3, 2020, YouTube video, 31:22, https://www.youtube.com/watch?v=5lCeWtXPKko.

10. "The History of the Pencil," British Library, May 28, 2019, https://blogs.bl.uk/untoldlives/2019/05/the-history-of-the-pencil.html; Megan Garber, "10 Things You Probably Did Not Know About Eraser Technology," *The Atlantic*, August 26, 2013, https://www.theatlantic.com/technology/archive/2013/08/10-things-you-probably-did-not-know-about-eraser-technology/279028/.

11. Joyce Meyer, "Start Saying the Right Things," Joyce Meyer Ministries, Facebook video, January 8, 2018, https://www.facebook.com/joycemeyerministries/videos/start-saying-the-right-things/10156177746662384/.

Chapter 20: The 5 *P*s Successful People Practice

1. Lisa Nichols, "These 3 Sentences Will Change Your Life," published by Goalcast on October 22, 2017, YouTube video, 8:03, https://www.youtube.com/watch?v=eWUs2QS1mJY.

Chapter 21: Get Your Megaphone Ready

1. "The Power of Words," published by The Power of Words on February 23, 2010, YouTube video, 1:47, https://www.youtube.com/watch?v=Hzgzim5m7oU&t=16s.

Chapter 22: You Have Something to Be Grateful For

1. John Kralik, *365 Thank Yous: The Year a Simple Act of Gratitude Changed My Life* (New York: Hachette, 2010).

2. Jack Canfield, "Using the Law of Attraction for Joy, Relationships, Money & More," Medium, December 13, 2018, https://medium.com /@officialjackcanfield/using-the-law-of-attraction-for-joy-relationships -money-more-8b782f23317f.

3. Heather Luszczyk, "The Toxic Effects of Complaining," Natural Healing News, February 28, 2012, https://naturalhealingnews.com /the-toxic-effects-of-complaining/.

Chapter 23: 5 Reasons Successful People Keep a Gratitude Journal

1. Paraphrased with slight detail changes from S. I. Kisher, "Appointment with Love," *Collier's Weekly*, June 5, 1943, 15.

2. "The Importance of Gratitude," UMass Dartmouth, accessed August 17, 2023, https://www.umassd.edu/counseling/for-parents /recommended-readings/the-importance-of-gratitude/.

3. Rainer Strack et al., "Decoding Global Talent: 200,000 Survey Responses on Global Mobility and Employment Preferences," BCG, October 6, 2014, https://www.bcg.com/publications/2014/people -organization-human-resources-decoding-global-talent.

4. Lemonade Journal, "Why Celebrities Keep a Gratitude Journal," Medium, July 16, 2020, https://medium.com /@lemonadejournalofficial/why-celebrities-keep-a-gratitude-journal -122c5c203bc7.

5. Cathy Hutchison, "Some of the Richest People Have Gratitude Practices. Should You?," Medium, August 12, 2018, https:// cathyhutchison.medium.com/some-of-the-richest-people-have -gratitude-practices-should-you-dc7a69f9003b.

6. Hutchison, "Some of the Richest People."

7. Gayle Thompson, "Brett Eldredge Explains Love of Gratitude Journaling," Pop Culture, July 6, 2018, https://popculture.com /country-music/news/brett-eldredge-explains-love-of-gratitude -journaling/.

8. Yoni Cohen, "5 Reasons Keeping a Gratitude Journal Will Change Your Life," GoodNet, August 1, 2017, https://www.goodnet.org /articles/5-reasons-keeping-gratitude-journal-will-change-your-life.

9. Allen M. Wood et al., "Gratitude Influences Sleep Through the Mechanism of Pre-Sleep Cognitions," *Journal of Psychosomatic Research*

66, no. 1 (January 2009): 43–48, https://doi.org/10.1016/j.jpsychores .2008.09.002.

10. David Horsager, "The Power of 90 Days," Trust Edge Leadership Institute, accessed August 18, 2023, https://davidhorsager.com/the -power-of-90-days/.

Chapter 24: Get God's Attention

1. Samantha Cortez, "Weird Jobs Celebs Had Before They Became Famous," *Insider*, July 26, 2012, https://www.businessinsider.com /weird-jobs-celebs-had-before-becoming-famous-2012–7.

Chapter 25: Give God What You've Got

1. Quoted in John Maxwell, *Be All That You Can Be: A Challenge to Stretch Your God-Given Potential* (Colorado Springs: David C. Cook, 2010), 36.

2. Kenneth Morris, "Sweet Victory," Sermons by Logos, accessed August 18, 2023, https://sermons.logos.com/sermons/93821-sweet -victory.

3. Paul Katzeef, "Basketball Player Larry Bird Grit and Discipline Helped Him Lead Championship Teams," *Investor's Business Daily*, January 31, 2001, https://www.investors.com/news/management /leaders-and-success/basketball-player-larry-bird-grit-and-discipline -helped-him-lead-championship-teams/.

4. Fred Schruers, "Jim Carrey: Bare Facts and Shocking Revelations," *Rolling Stone*, July 13, 1995, https://www.rollingstone.com/culture /culture-news/jim-carrey-bare-facts-and-shocking-revelations -181569/.

5. "Michael Jordan: Turning Weakness into Strength," *CorD Magazine*, no. 173 (February 2019), 49, https://issuu.com/cordmagazines/docs /bd_173_small/s/73215.

6. Tom Vitale, "Winston Churchill's Way with Words," NPR, July 14, 2012, transcript, https://www.npr.org/2012/07/14/156720829 /winston-churchills-way-with-words.

7. Vladimir Horowitz, quoted in Geoffrey Colvin, "What It Takes to Be Great," CNN, October 30, 2006, https://money.cnn.com/magazines /fortune/fortune_archive/2006/10/30/8391794/index.htm.

Chapter 26: 5 Things Successful People Quit

1. "The Motivational Success Story of Denzel Washington—From Poor Garbage Man to Oscar Winner," published by Inspire Yourself on April 18, 2019, YouTube video, 6:51, https://www.youtube.com/watch?v=s5Q3jtOZFWw.

2. Joel Osteen, *Become a Better You: 7 Keys for Improving Your Life Every Day* (New York: Free Press, 2017), 11.

3. Jessie Kratz, "The Great Seal: Celebrating 233 Years of a National Emblem," National Archives, *Pieces of History* (blog), June 20, 2015, https://prologue.blogs.archives.gov/2015/06/20/the-great-seal-celebrating-233-years-of-a-national-emblem/.

4. Zig Ziglar, *See You at the Top*, 25th anniversary ed. (Gretna, LA: Pelican Publishing, 2000), 69.

5. Eliana Dockterman, "Facebook Once Turned Down WhatsApp Founder for a Job," *TIME*, February 20, 2014, https://techland.time.com/2014/02/20/facebook-whatsapp-brian-acton-job/; "Brian Acton Biography," The Famous People, accessed June 2, 2023, https://www.thefamouspeople.com/profiles/brian-acton-42144.php.

6. Ziglar, *See You at the Top*, 231.

7. Ken Dunn, "5 Self-Publishing Book Tips from the 'Chicken Soup for the Soul' Author Who Has Sold Over 500 Million Copies," *Entrepreneur*, July 29, 2020, https://www.entrepreneur.com/growing-a-business/5-self-publishing-book-tips-from-the-chicken-soup-for-the/352513.

8. Rachel Chang, "Dr. Seuss Wrote 'Green Eggs and Ham' on a Bet," Biography, March 2, 2020, https://www.biography.com/authors-writers/dr-seuss-green-eggs-and-ham-bet.

9. Eudie Pak, "Walt Disney's Rocky Road to Success," Biography, Jun 17, 2020, https://www.biography.com/movies-tv/walt-disney-failures.

10. Keith Craft, "Choose Your Hard," Warrior Night, Elevate Life Church, Frisco, Texas, May 16, 2019.

Chapter 27: Get Ready!

1. Shonda Rimes, *Year of Yes* (New York: Simon & Schuster, 2015), 2.

2. Tom Ward, "The Amazing Story of the Making of 'Rocky,'" *Forbes*, August 29, 2017, https://www.forbes.com/sites/tomward/2017/08/29/the-amazing-story-of-the-making-of-rocky/?sh=556c8cbc560b.

3. John C. Maxwell, "Do It Now," *Dallas Business Journal*, updated October 3, 2004, https://www.bizjournals.com/dallas/stories/2004/10/04/smallb3.html.

Chapter 28: Have You Had Enough?

1. Jen Juneau, "Tina Turner Revealed Harrowing Night She Escaped Ike Turner's Abuse: 'I Was Living a Life of Death' (Exclusive)," *People*, updated May 25, 2023, https://people.com/tina-turner-recalled-escaping-ike-turner-abusive-marriage-1981-people-interview-7503995.
2. Jim Rohn, "The Four Emotions That Can Lead to Life Change," Get Motivation, accessed August 22, 2023, https://www.getmotivation.com/jimrohn/jr4emotions.html.
3. "Wilma Rudolph: A Trio of Golds Against All Odds," Olympics (website), updated June 27, 2023, https://olympics.com/en/news/wilma-rudolpha-the-trio-of-golds.

Chapter 29: 3 Decisions Successful People Make

1. Geraldine Fabrikant, "Talking Money with: Sarah Jessica Parker; From a Start on Welfare to Riches in the City," *New York Times*, July 30, 2000, https://www.nytimes.com/2000/07/30/business/talking-money-with-sarah-jessica-parker-start-welfare-riches-city.html.
2. "Sarah Jessica Parker Net Worth: $200 Million," Celebrity Net Worth, last updated May 8, 2023, https://www.celebritynetworth.com/richest-celebrities/actors/sarah-jessica-parker-net-worth/. Between television and film salaries, Sarah Jessica Parker earned $250 million from HBO thanks to *Sex and the City*. Nothing for Carrie Bradshaw as she's a fictional character.
3. Sarah Jessica Parker, "Exclusive: Sarah Jessica Parker Reminisces on Her First Love: The Ballet," published by *Entertainment Tonight* on October 31, 2014, YouTube video, 2:05, https://www.youtube.com/watch?v=RT9R6c_5Dy4.
4. Joyce Meyer, "Waiting for Your Miracle?," Joyce Meyer Ministries, Facebook video, August 10, 2018, https://www.facebook.com/joycemeyerministries/videos/waiting-for-your-miracle/10156718475132384/.
5. Brian Tracy, *Maximum Achievement: Strategies and Skills That Will*

Unlock Your Hidden Powers to Succeed (New York: Simon & Schuster, 1993), 94–95.

6. John Assaraf and Murray Smith, *The Answer: Grow Any Business, Achieve Financial Freedom, and Live an Extraordinary Life* (New York: Atria Books, 2008), 50.

7. "Decision (n.)," *Online Etymology Dictionary*, accessed August 22, 2023, https://www.etymonline.com/word/decision.

Chapter 30: Get Your Obituary Ready!

1. Bob Proctor, "It's About Time to Stop Wasting Your Time!," published by Proctor Gallagher on February 28, 2020, YouTube video, 6:15, https://www.youtube.com/watch?v=BJlh-Nu0c14.

2. Joel Osteen, *Become a Better You: 7 Keys to Improving Your Live Every Day* (New York: Free Press, 2007), 71.

3. John Maxwell, *The Greatest Story Ever Told* (New York: Center Street, 2016), back cover.

About the Author

Terri Savelle Foy is known as the cheerleader of dreams. The founder of an international Christian ministry and the host of the *Live Your Dreams* television broadcast, she is also a best-selling author, conference speaker, and success coach to hundreds of thousands of people all over the world.

For years Terri's life was average. She had no dreams to pursue. Finally, with a marriage in trouble and her life falling apart, she began to pursue God like never before and developed a new routine. As she started to recognize and write down her dreams and goals, that written vision became a road map to drive her life, and those dreams are now a reality.

Her bestselling books—*5 Things Successful People Do Before 8am*, *Imagine Big*, and *Pep Talk*—weekly podcast, YouTube channel, and coaching courses are a lifeline of hope and inspiration. She is convinced that "if you can dream it, God can do it." Known as a motivator of hope and success through her transparent and humorous teaching style—and of course, her hilarious props—Terri's unique ability to communicate success strategies in a simple and practical way has awakened the dreams of the young and old alike.

Terri and her husband, Rodney, have been married since 1991 and are the proud parents of one beautiful daughter, Kassidi Cherie. They live near Dallas, Texas. For more information about Terri, go to www.terri.com.